How to Leave the Church

GRETE RACHEL HOWLAND

APOCRYPHILE
PRESS

Apocryphile Press
PO Box 255
Hannacroix, NY 12087
www.apocryphilepress.com

Copyright © 2024 by Grete Rachel Howland
Printed in the United States of America
ISBN 978-1-958061-75-6 | paper
ISBN 978-1-958061-76-3 | ePub

No part of this book may be reproduced, stored in a retrieval system, or transmitted in any form or by any means electronic, mechanical, photocopy, recording, or otherwise without written permission of the author and publisher, except for brief quotations in printed reviews.

Please join our mailing list at www.apocryphilepress.com/free
We'll keep you up-to-date on all our new releases,
and we'll also send you a FREE BOOK.
Visit us today!

For my younger self

Sometimes in life the foundation upon which one stands will give a tilt, and everything that one has previously believed and held dear will begin sliding about, and suddenly all things will seem strange and new.
—George Saunders, *Ghoul*

Now that you don't have to be perfect, you can be good.
—John Steinbeck, *East of Eden*

CONTENTS

Author's Note	ix
Introduction	xiii
Step 1 *Pay Attention to Your Doubt*	1
Step 2 *Get Angry with God*	22
Step 3 *Make Friends with Sinners*	59
Step 4 *Study the Bible*	82
Step 5 *Keep Your Eyes Open in Church*	106
Step 6 *Ask the Big Questions*	129
Step 7 *Let It Go*	147
Epilogue	172
Acknowledgements	179

AUTHOR'S NOTE

I began this book with two groups of people in mind: those who are wondering if they want to identify as Christians anymore, and those who have already decided that they don't. I wanted to write something to say that you do have permission to leave the church. Even if your friends won't understand, even if you know all the folks who helped raise you will be disappointed. Leaving might not be easy, but Christianity is not something you have to keep participating in if you don't believe what they believe anymore, or if it hurts you or the people you love.

I also wrote this book to let you know that you will not be alone if you leave. Yes, you might lose a reliable community—maybe your primary community—because community is something the church is actually pretty good at (assuming you're willing to play by its rules). And it could be that some people with whom you used to be close will not want to keep in touch at all. Even those relationships with other Christians that aren't totally severed by your departure might end up feeling diminished, regardless of your love for each other.

AUTHOR'S NOTE

These facts warrant grieving. But also, it's going to be okay. There are a lot of us former Christians out there, and most of us are happy to talk about what it's like to walk this road. One thing I can testify to—aside from the fact that a word like "testify" starts to feel a bit sour on the tongue once you've left the fold—is that it's worth it to follow your heart, even if it leads you into unknown territory. Difficult feelings and situations will arise as a result; still, I suspect that knowing you're not pretending to believe anymore—if you were pretending even for a moment—will quickly become something you wouldn't trade for all the false security in the world. I know I wouldn't.

What follows here is, in essence, the story of how I decided I was done with the church. In many ways this story is uniquely mine. For instance, it is important to note the limits of my experience in and with the church given that I am an able-bodied white woman who's always been both sexually and romantically attracted to men. My stories hardly represent every church, let alone every Christian, and they are not necessarily an indictment of Christianity as a whole. I can only speak for myself. Nevertheless, I want to offer an example of what this kind of journey can, and often does, involve.

I'll also add a couple of notes here about some of the terminology in the book. First, I use "church," "the church," and "Christianity" mostly interchangeably. Not everyone sees these things as one and the same. For example, I know many people self-identifying as Christians who are just not interested in attending an organized church, or who condemn what institutionalized Christianity has become. For me,

AUTHOR'S NOTE

though, leaving the church meant leaving the religion, and vice versa. Occasionally, I do refer to a particular congregation or church building; I hope that distinction will be clear from the context.

Second, you might notice that I use capitalized male pronouns to refer to God, such as "He." While I now disagree with this gendering of God and find the capitalization practice a bit ridiculous, I chose to refer to God in this way because it reflects the very specific understanding of God that I was raised with, and it's how I thought of God when I was going through the experiences described here. Doing so also helps distinguish between God and other people who use he/him/his pronouns who show up in my story.

Books have the power to bring together individuals who are otherwise separated by time and space. Reading others' stories of questioning and deconversion was a significant comfort to me as I made my way on this journey. My most strongly felt wish for this book is that even one person struggling with what to do about their religion finds companionship, understanding, and maybe a little courage in its pages.

With hope and love,
Grete Rachel Howland
2024

INTRODUCTION

I came by my Christianity honestly.

My religious career began when I was an infant, wailing in the church's nursery every Sunday while my mother attended service in the building next door.

On top of my weekly church attendance, I went to a conservative Baptist elementary school from preschool until fourth grade, at which point my parents switched me and my younger sister over to public education. To give you an idea of what I mean by "conservative," the school, which met on the campus of another church in town that we weren't otherwise involved in, was not afraid to ban books. I found this out when the faculty and parents agreed to remove the entire *Baby-Sitters Club* series from the already anemic library collection that they housed in a small utility room in the basement. I have no idea why they decided to cast out the series—it was deemed to be a bad influence by someone, somehow. To my own parents' credit, I remember them scoffing and rolling their eyes when they spoke of the scandal at home.

Such early encounters with traditional Christian interests

INTRODUCTION

weren't limited to my nuclear family or primary education, either. All of my relatives—every grandparent, aunt, uncle, and cousin—were believers, at least as far as I could tell. I even had an uncle who was an ordained pastor; he, my aunt, and my cousins spent a number of years living in Ghana as missionaries when I was young. There was not a family function I went to that didn't involve prayer in one way or another, plus frequent mentions of God, heaven, some distant relative I'd never met who recently died now being with God in heaven, and guardian angels.

I'd been swimming in the faith since birth, and I had recommitted my life to God on a constant basis throughout my childhood and adolescence, perpetually afraid that my ticket to heaven had somehow been revoked without my knowing it. Because of all this, I never had a single, dramatic moment of conversion to speak of. The closest thing to it—the day I would always count as my official entry into the fold, if I had to choose one—happened one morning when I was in kindergarten.

Our teacher that year was a woman I presumed to be elderly because she had short gray hair. (But children can't be trusted to determine adults' ages, so who knows how old she actually was?) On the day in question, she decided the time had come to present all of her young charges with the opportunity to be saved. Not completely aware of the implications of what I was about to do, but also understanding that this was somehow very important, I decided to take her up on the offer. Sitting cross-legged on the carpet in a circle with the rest of my tiny classmates, I tried my best to keep my eyes closed while I followed her instructions and said the magic words: "Dear Jesus, please come into my heart."

Suddenly, there I was, permanently forgiven.

Forgiven for what, I wasn't quite sure. I didn't feel

anything inside of me change. No one in the room seemed to notice anything different about me, either. When our prayer time was over, the teacher moved us from the carpet to our desks, just like she did every other day, and we went on with our lessons. All I knew was that I'd done what I understood to be necessary based on the theology I'd already absorbed, even at five years old.

It wasn't until I started going to youth group in the seventh grade that I began to wish my testimony had a little more edge to it, that I had bothered to do some things wrong before dedicating my whole life to being a good Christian.

All through middle and high school, youth pastors would bring in speakers with seedy pasts who told of near-death experiences and lives saved from impending destruction only after total submission to God. Most of the stories had to do with addiction, which was always framed as a moral failing. And in every case, it was some supernatural experience—an audible voice from the ether, or even the literal appearance of a heavenly being before the subject's very eyes—that revealed God's loving presence to the person in their hour of need and convinced them to turn their life around.

Even kids my age got up now and then to share about their own pre-Jesus prodigal adventures. They spoke awkwardly about their sexual exploits (exploits that, I can see now, would be pretty run-of-the-mill for teenagers in a secular context) and experiments with underage drinking. They admitted that even though it probably looked like they were having fun partying, the truth was they were miserable on the inside, and no amount of hooking up or getting drunk or high made it better. Church was where they finally found

INTRODUCTION

healing and joy, they said; God was the only one who filled the void inside their souls.

Their witness was inspiring, and I wanted to be inspiring too. But I had no past to make up for, no previous dark deeds to run from. My decision to follow Jesus happened before I was old enough to do basic arithmetic, let alone skip school to smoke in the parking lot. My testimony was boring, and there are few things more disappointing for a young evangelical Christian than having a boring testimony. I came into this world the child of churchgoing, Bible-believing parents, and I was an obedient kid to boot. There was little I could do to hide the fact that I'd never really known or done anything other than what I was supposed to.

Well, almost.

There was one hidden shame. This wasn't the everyday, baseline remorse that comes from being told early and often about the inescapable ugliness of your inherent sin. No, I'm talking about the acute, sometimes anxiety attack-inducing feeling of guilt that comes from being a teenage Christian girl with a sex drive. A teenage Christian girl who masturbates.

Boys weren't supposed to be touching themselves either, of course, but it was implied—and sometimes explicitly stated—by our pastors and preachers that that was just going to happen. How could they help themselves? Their libido was, to a certain extent, uncontrollable. It was simply a fact of life that they would slip up in this area. Nothing a good accountability group session couldn't take care of.

That's not to say that the boys I went to church with weren't also ashamed of masturbating. They were certainly told to *try* to control themselves, and I know many who dealt with heavy guilt around their own carnal urges well into adulthood. But at least the act was talked about as a reality of

INTRODUCTION

everyday adolescent experience. For us girls, it was simply never mentioned.

In all the lectures about sexual purity I heard over the course of my many years in youth group, not once did an adult acknowledge the fact that a young woman would (or even physically could) masturbate. That silence—that tacit, insidious communication about what was supposedly normal and what was deviant—taught me that a woman's role, biologically and socially, was to be the receiver of a man's erotic passion. That it was our job to wait around until *they* wanted to have sex with *us*, and then make sure to hold them off until marriage. The binary was clear.

It took me all the way until college just to learn that I wasn't the only Christian girl out there who got horny. I suffered in darkness, literally. I thought I was a pervert. And one of the most frustrating parts of it all was that I could never turn the struggle into a testimony. I could never find support and admiration by sharing the story of my shame. How would it look for me, an already devout follower of Christ, to admit that I'd been secretly sinning for all those years and still couldn't stop? Plus, my sin wasn't cool like partying; my sin was gross and weird and embarrassing.

In the end, the utter disgrace of my actions far outweighed my desire to have an inspiring tale to tell, so I kept my story to myself despite my yearning to have something meaningful to share with my fellow believers. Truthfully—and I do mean truthfully—I would rather have died than admit my perpetual transgression to anyone, let alone a crowd.

Despite how heavily my contemptible deed weighed on me in certain moments—like during group prayer sessions, when we were invited to confess our sins to the Lord in the quietness of our own hearts, and I was suddenly terrified that everyone around me could somehow read my mind—it wasn't always at the forefront of my consciousness. There were enough fun games and compelling discussions happening each week at youth group that I spent a good amount of my time there distracted from my various teenage worries rather than caught up in them.

When it came down to it, despite the fact that it was my religion that designated my sexual urges as impure, I didn't ever associate church with shame, which was both a blessing and a curse, depending on how you look at it. Church was a safe space for me, a shy and uncool kid. In general, other than the aforementioned aberration, I was good at being a Christian, and being good made me feel great. Still, the truth was that I did have to bury a part of myself very deep in order to fully enjoy myself there—a part of myself that, in another context, I might have learned to cherish and embrace.

Ultimately, this was the tale of my faith, all the way into my mid-twenties: It was a garment that fit me well, and I wore it with pride daily, yet there were secret stains that marred its inner lining. It was easy enough to keep other people from seeing those blemishes, so I got through the days with what probably looked like ease. At the same time, I lived in constant, unacknowledged embarrassment for being unable to maintain perfection underneath the outer shell.

It was a torturous cycle. I felt horrifically guilty for masturbating because the church, the place I loved, taught me it was dirty. My response was then to cling to the church even tighter, because it offered me freedom from my guilt at the same time that it accused me. The problem was not the church, as far as I was concerned. The problem was me. And as long as I believed that, I had no issue with the rules that were causing me so much grief.

INTRODUCTION

Forgiveness and condemnation, acceptance and exile, freedom and being completely controlled—all of these things are offered and insisted upon by the Christianity in which I grew up. Each element needing its opposite. Each dichotomy originating from within the doctrine itself (despite what the people in charge might say). Each person daily pleading for their life from the God who, they are told, both loves them with a love beyond all understanding, but who also can't stand the sight of them if they're going to keep screwing up all the time.

It sounds terrible, and eventually I realized it was. But it was also normal for me. I couldn't see my religion as the incongruous, manipulative thing I'm describing now—and it was not because of a lack of intelligence, as so many loud-mouthed, arrogant secularists like to insist. Rather, what I lacked was luck. The luck of sufficient exposure to a diversity of ideas. The luck of a personality brave and confident enough to shuck the inherited identity that gave me safety and belonging in a life where I felt like I never quite fit in.

As far as I knew—and I never had the chance to know any different—Christianity gave me what I needed. Unfortunately, what I wasn't aware of, and what it took me until adulthood to comprehend, was how many of the needs I thought I had were actually being manufactured by the church itself.

I did get lucky eventually: I was spared success in a romantic relationship that might have solidified my life-long presence in the evangelical church. I stumbled upon friendships that demonstrated the joy of living in what I had been told was sin. And I happened to find myself in theology classes with professors just free-thinking enough to present

INTRODUCTION

the possibility that something I'd been told my whole life could be wrong, even something coming from the church.

All of these things, which I'll describe in detail soon because that is the point of this book, were my true salvation. They led me to my deconversion, and *that* story—this heretic's testimony—is one I could not be more proud of.

STEP 1
PAY ATTENTION TO YOUR DOUBT

I was nine years old when my parents first sent me to a week-long sleepaway summer camp nestled in the redwood forest, a windy twenty-minute drive inland from where we lived on the central California coast.

This wasn't just any camp. This camp, which was specifically for elementary-aged kids, was one third of a larger Christian retreat center that also included a separate camp for middle and high school students and a family camp. All three properties were situated along a wooded hillside, with the adolescent camp at the top, the family camp in the middle, and the elementary camp at the bottom, closest to the dammed-up creek where people of all ages would hike and go boating during the day. And this whole operation, every element included, was more or less responsible for the formation of my household as I knew it.

It started with my maternal grandmother, Gerda. After emigrating from Germany to the U.S. with my mother and uncle in the late 1950s and making her way west, she took a job as a housekeeper for the family camp facilities. Persisting through prejudice and poverty, she stayed there for two decades before retiring as head of the department.

My mother herself became a receptionist in the family camp's main office when she was in her early twenties, while at the same time my dad, who grew up in a different part of the state, accepted an internship at the adolescent camp. His decision to take the job was significant—for him, her, and me—because this is how my parents met. The first time my father saw my mother was at the annual summer staff welcome banquet. According to family legend (a legend of which my father is the sole proprietor) his first words after catching a glimpse of her during group introductions were, "Wow, what a fox!"

This place kept my family going, financially, biologically, and—for better or worse—spiritually. It is thanks to this place that one side of my family had enough to get by, and it is thanks to this place that I am even alive. It is also thanks to this place, where I too worked the summers during my college years, that I had a place where I felt included and special in the midst of a childhood in which I often felt awkward and isolated. And it is thanks to this place and all of the import it held in my mind that I happily ingested religious instruction so alarming that it would haunt me through high school and beyond and test the limits of my commitment to a Christianity rooted in judgment and shame.

IT ALL STARTED out quite fun. The elementary level facilities where I began my journey as a camper presented an adventure in the rustic. I remember concrete-floored cabins with no attached bathrooms (I understand they've since been renovated) lit dimly by a single long fluorescent tube affixed to the center of the ceiling. Four dark-stained and sturdy wood-framed bunk sets lined the bare interior walls, which created enough space for seven campers and one counselor. Each bed was cushioned with a nylon-covered mattress that would stick to whatever part of your skin wasn't tucked inside your sleeping bag. I recall the cabins always smelling like soil and sequoia bark with a hint of mildew from drying towels and swimsuits hanging on a clothesline just outside the front door. This particular potpourri marked the highlight of my summers, and I loved it.

Our mornings and afternoons were spent as you'd expect: hiking through the woods, paddling canoes, playing capture the flag, feeding the small herd of goats that were inexplicably kept in a log enclosure at the edge of the main field, and making classic summer camp crafts like tie-dyed t-shirts and friendship bracelets.

Because this was a Christian camp, we also had a quiet solo time with God every day. Personally, I liked to spend those thirty minutes sitting in the dirt with my back against a tree's rough trunk while I read my Bible (a required item on the packing list), wrote in my journal, or just stared off into the distance for a while.

Each day culminated with an evening gathering where we all sang worship songs, laughed at some corny skits, and heard a story or two that usually illustrated a basic Biblical principle like the fact that God loved us all unconditionally or how we should be nice to everyone whether we felt like it or not.

That was the camp experience I grew used to, the one I got excited for as summer approached. Even the long walk from the cabins to the bathrooms and the anxiety of meeting a whole new group of people every year couldn't put me off. Until I hit puberty, that is. Things changed a bit then—as they tend to do—and the first summer I spent at camp as a full-blown adolescent turned out to be the last one I'd spend there as a camper ever again.

IT WAS the summer that preceded my ninth-grade year. For some reason that I can't now remember, I did not attend camp while in the throes of middle school. Maybe money was tight; maybe I wanted a break from the things of my childhood, per the typical inclination of that age.

In any case, that meant I'd missed the experience of moving up to the adolescent campus with the rest of my cohort just before we all entered seventh grade. So this, my final summer, was also my first time encountering the premises that other campers of my grade level had eased into over the past two years. It didn't take long to see that the experience was going to be different than what I was used to in a few significant ways.

The first thing that surprised me about the unfamiliar grounds was the cabins. Apparently, adolescent campers were more deserving of amenities than elementary school kids—or perhaps more prone to complain about not having them—because these cabins were much nicer than what I'd known before. They were well-lit, carpeted, smelled like cleaning chemicals, and had (what seemed to me at the time) lavishly large bathrooms that were, to my great delight, actually attached to the structure in which we were sleeping.

Then there was the evening meeting space. As elementary-age campers, we spent twilight outdoors, bundled up in hoodies and huddled together on wooden bleachers that curved around a concrete stage with the surrounding forest serving as a natural backdrop. Here at the high school level, we moved inside. No more shivering or swatting away bugs for an hour before bed. Instead, we basked in the warm glory of a spacious, indoor amphitheater. We spread our bodies out on shallow tiers of carpeted floor that cascaded gently down the length of the rectangular room toward the stage area, where guitars and microphones were always set up and ready to go. Behind the audio equipment, a large projector screen hung from the ceiling, waiting to show us photos of our daily activities, song lyrics, or maybe a video that the counselors had made. These end-of-day assemblies were a modern, multimedia affair.

They were also the venue for the final and most striking difference between the camp experience I'd grown used to as a child and the one I'd suddenly graduated into as a soon-to-be freshman. That difference was in the programming. Granted, the daylight hours themselves were spent in pretty familiar ways—field games, a ropes course, boating, swimming, and so on. But it was the end-of-day gatherings, which had been nothing if not lighthearted just a couple years before, where unexpected things began to happen. The content became, shall we say, more mature.

Specifically, the skits got way more intense. No longer were they the silly, gag-filled things we'd known as children, meant to get our giggles out before bedtime while simultaneously reinforcing the simplest of Sunday school lessons. No, at the high school level, it would seem that exhausting us in preparation for a good night's sleep was no longer the primary purpose of the scripts the counselors enacted, nor were they going to settle for uncomplicated stories of a feel-good Jesus anymore. At the high school level, there were scare tactics involved.

I can still picture the night when things turned serious. It all started out innocuously. The cabin groups streamed eagerly into the meeting room after dinner and whatever sunset game the counselors had planned for us that evening. We made ourselves comfortable on the floor, just as we did every time we found ourselves in that space. And, just as they did every night, the adults (or those who seemed to be adults; in reality, many of them were probably still college students) made sure we weren't sitting for too long. Before we knew it, guitar straps were being slung over counselors' heads and we were on our feet, singing and clapping and doing the accompanying hand-motions to the lyrics we seasoned campers knew by heart. Sure we were going to start ninth grade in a few weeks, but we were still young enough to be coaxed into a little goofiness now and then.

Eventually the music died down, and we thought we knew what to expect next: a skit that was sure to have some moral to it, put on by a few theatrically inclined counselors. That would then be followed by a short, meant-to-be poignant message from another counselor or maybe even the camp director, and finally we'd be released to our bunks for the night. It was a fun but unremarkable routine.

Until this evening, that is. This evening, we witnessed something truly provocative—and truly unnerving. So unnerving, in fact, that of all the skits I saw in all the weeks I went to camp from elementary school until ninth grade, it's the only one I really remember.

ONCE THE GUITARS were returned to their stands and the sounds of our whispered conversations faded to something close to silence, two female counselors walked wordlessly in from the back of the room. Not everyone noticed them at first, but heads started to turn as they made their way through the center of the audience and, eventually, down to the stage. As they walked, they looked around the room, their exaggerated body language communicating that they were pretending to be in a place neither of them had seen before.

Once they both reached the center of the stage, they stopped and stood just a few feet apart from each other. They continued to look around the room, apparently for some clue as to where they were. Their affectation indicated that this place was not only new to them but also, somehow, wondrous.

After a few more beats of dramatized bewilderment, they turned toward each other. The woman who stood to the right as you faced the stage—I'll call her Jane—asked, "Where are we?"

"I think...we're dead," said the woman on the left—let's name her Cindy. "We were driving. Then the last thing I remember is that truck coming toward us in the intersection."

"Oh man," Jane said, taking a moment to process what was happening. They both continued to look around the otherwise empty stage. "What happens now?"

On cue, a male counselor-turned-actor, dressed in a white choir robe, appeared behind Cindy. He gently said her name, so quietly that we could barely hear it, and she turned her body toward him in response. "It's time to go," he said, smiling.

"Who's that?" Jane asked.

"I...I think it's an angel."

"Are you ready? He's waiting for you," the angel said warmly.

Cindy began to smile knowingly and took a step in the direction toward which the angel was gesturing. The direction, incidentally, that would lead her away from her friend.

"Wait, can I come too? I want to come," Jane said hopefully, clearly not wanting to be left alone.

Cindy turned back toward the friend she was about to leave behind. "Are you a Christian?" she asked, also somewhat hopefully.

"Well, no, I don't think so."

"You can't get into heaven if you aren't a Christian," Cindy said with pity in her voice.

"Okay, well, how do I become a Christian? I'll do it right now."

"You just have to ask Jesus into your heart. But it's too late. You have to do it while you're still alive."

"How come you never told me about this?" Jane's tone moved quickly from hopeful to panicked. "You knew and you never told me?"

"I'm sorry. I thought you wouldn't want to hear it," Cindy said with a mixture of sadness and defensiveness. "I didn't want to offend you or make you feel judged. I didn't want to risk losing you as a friend."

"But what am I supposed to do now? I thought you cared about me," said Jane. She sounded like she was about to cry as she came to terms with the terrible reality of her situation.

"I'm so sorry," Cindy said. She seemed remorseful but made no move to comfort her friend. "I have to go now."

She turned and walked offstage with the angel, who seemed eerily unmoved by the small tragedy that had just unfolded before him.

As Cindy departed, leaving her friend alone in this otherworldly space, we turned our attention back to Jane, only to notice that a new character had walked up behind her from her side of the stage. He was dressed all in black and had a sinister look on his face. If the other young man was an angel, it was clear that this one was meant to be a demon.

Rather than holding out an open hand to her in eager invitation, he wordlessly directed her offstage with an extended arm and pointed finger. There was nothing welcoming about his stance. Jane hung her head and walked slowly in the direction toward which he was pointing. He followed behind her, grinning menacingly, as we the audience sat in heavy silence.

LOOKING BACK NOW—HAVING spent a number of years learning what the secular world considers normal, and still in the midst of processing a good amount of anger toward the evangelical church—I know I should be completely horrified that fourteen-year-old me had to sit through that skit. I should be horrified that any child would have to sit through it, as I'm sure they are still being made to do at Christian camps all across the world. Yet if I'm honest, when I retell it, I feel more nostalgia than horror. I even feel—though I know it is twisted of me—kind of inspired.

I guess I'm remembering what it felt like then. And back then, in the moment, before the ramifications of what I'd witnessed became apparent to me, I ate up every second of it. It was melodramatic. It was tragic. It expressed frantic emotions that felt akin to those churning inside my pubescent body every second of every day. It drew me in with all of that and then also reinforced the intense cosmic significance of the religious group to which I belonged. It was a pill specially coated for people my age to swallow in the hopes of imbuing us with at least a couple of different ideas.

First and most obviously was the idea that there is no excuse that will keep a person out of hell if they have not accepted Jesus Christ as their personal Lord and Savior. You say your Christian friend was too scared or too lazy to tell you about the Good News? Too bad. Even people in the so-called "unreached" (read: uncolonized) corners of the globe who have no chance of knowing about Christianity from any source other than missionaries will not be off the hook when it comes to the afterlife. How much more accountable do you think God will hold those who grow up surrounded by Christianized culture? Ignorance, in this case, will not be bliss.

I already knew all of that, of course, and had secured my salvation accordingly many years prior. It was the second idea that the skit communicated that I found significantly more poignant. This idea was a bit more advanced, perhaps more geared toward those of us who were already believers. It stuck with me insidiously, in some unconscious place I couldn't name until much later. The idea was that it would be my own fault if my friends went to hell, and boy did I take it to heart once I started high school.

There were multiple occasions on which I found myself trying to argue my closest comrades out of their own non-Christian religions or their atheism, even as they showed visible signs of exasperation, or sometimes even rage. I invited just about every acquaintance I ever had to youth group in the hopes that they would find the kind of belonging there that I did and be saved. I even went so far as to literally tell a coworker at one mind-numbing summer retail job that she was going to hell. In fairness to my younger self, she asked.

None of it ever worked, of course. I could find no compelling reason for these people to change their ways of thinking. I had no actual argument up my sleeve. Every Christian spiel that came out of my mouth must have sounded ridiculous to those who hadn't been raised with Bible stories since birth (or witnessed profoundly troubling skits at Christian summer camp). I can see now, so clearly, that there was no truth in my words for anyone I talked to, only the desperation of my needing them not to die unsaved—of knowing it would be my fault, somehow, if they didn't get into heaven.

But did I know it? That x-factor of "somehow" was a lot of mystery to swallow, especially with the possibility of infinite remorse on the line. Indeed, there was a small part of me that perceived that something was suspicious about a logic that would drive me to browbeat my dearest friends with put-downs of their own belief systems out of fear that I would end up spending eternity with a guilty conscience.

If nothing else, the responsibility just felt like too much sometimes; it left me anxious and wracked with a sense of perpetual failure. I couldn't help but wonder if that was really what God wanted for me. Now and then, when I wasn't caught up in the adrenaline of theological debate, I had my doubts.

The strict entrance policy for heaven was another thing I couldn't quite explain, to myself or anybody else. Despite my genuine, ardent commitment to the ideas I was preaching, there was something in me that understood why I kept getting the brush-off whenever I started sharing the Gospel. There was a part of me that knew that the fundamentalist Christian narrative—the one that said that this particular story was the only story that could keep you from an eternity of suffering—didn't make sense. There was a part of me that knew I was working with absurd material.

The question was what to do with that part, and my answer—unfortunately but understandably—was to ignore it. To shrug it off. I refused to grant the possibility of its legitimacy. Because what if that doubt was a trick? What if that gently nagging feeling that there were easier and more enjoyable ways of looking at the universe was just Satan trying to lure me off the righteous path? People's lives were at stake. The risk involved in not following this deeply urgent evangelical lifestyle, should it prove true in the end, was too great.

So—at least at that point in my life, when I was still terrified of authority and desperate to keep the loving arms of the church wrapped around me—I stuck to the script I'd been handed, even it if meant refusing to acknowledge how ludicrous (and often hurtful) my position was. Plus, it was all I knew. Being the zealous Christian girl was not an endearing or popular identity to have, but it was an identity nonetheless. And when you're in high school, maintaining an identity is simply more important than following logic.

THE GOSPEL NARRATIVE I grew up with—that is, the narrative of humanity's inherent sin relieved only through Christianity's exclusive ability to grant individuals salvation from eternal torment—and the dire obligation to share it with everyone I knew were not the only parts of my religious experience that sometimes felt a little off. Nor was my post-summer camp proselytizing phase the first time I felt vaguely uncomfortable with what my religion was asking me to take on. There were a number of things I heard at church in my youth, whether in an official capacity from the pulpit or just mentioned casually by some fellow congregant, that didn't make sense to me.

I remember that the question of creation versus evolution came up at some point in my early years. I don't know if our church held to something as hardcore as Young Earth Creationism, which says that the world was created in just six days no more than ten thousand years ago, but I did glean from somewhere when I was a child that there was indeed a discrepancy between what the Bible said about how this universe came to be and what science told us was the source of all existence.

Trying to arrive at a satisfying solution, one day—I must have been in fourth or fifth grade—I asked my mother, herself a devout believer, about dinosaurs and fossils and all of the things that seemed to me to be pretty hard evidence suggesting there was more to the history of our world than the first two chapters of Genesis. She listened attentively and agreed that my observations were good ones. She floated the idea that God might have used evolution to bring about the world we know today. There might have even been an acknowledgement on her part of the possibility that the authors of the Biblical creation story were working with metaphor. Only in retrospect do I fully appreciate how valuable this moment was and what I learned about the potential that existed for negotiating with the church, even if I was so young that the lesson was taken in unconsciously.

It was a similar story with what I'll call the Catholic Problem. The Baptist denomination in which I grew up, like many Protestant communities, denounced Catholicism as false Christianity. I was taught that Catholics weren't real Christians because they worshipped Mary and... Well, that was the extent of the justification I remember hearing. I assume the grown-ups around me had plenty of other criticisms to throw down; I just didn't happen to absorb them in any way that stuck with me. Regardless, there was something about this judgment of Catholics that felt harsh and unfair to me. I don't think I knew any practicing Catholics until my late teens, but I felt some kind of empathy for their tradition nonetheless.

Once again, I brought my confusion to my mother. For some reason, I remember this brief conversation—which happened when I was in middle school—in great detail. We were driving in our rust-colored Oldsmobile station wagon through a town just north of the one we lived in. The velvety headliner of the car had started detaching from the middle of the ceiling not long after we bought it, and I could see the dangling fabric in my peripheral vision. I don't know what made me think of it, but the Catholic Problem popped into my mind at that moment, and I felt like voicing my concern.

"Catholics still believe that Jesus was the son of God, and that he died and rose again, right?" I asked from the passenger seat. From my mother's perspective, I assume the question came out of left field, but she dove in with me like always.

"Yes," she replied.

"Well, then, how can they not be Christians? Even if they worship Mary, they still believe the most important thing, the thing that gets you into Heaven. Isn't that the definition of a Christian?"

"It is, and Catholics do believe in Jesus," she concurred. She went on to explain that it's not really anyone's place to judge the faith of another person, and that only God knows our hearts. I don't remember where our conversation went after that, but I do know that, as with my questions about the discrepancy between creation and evolution, I left the discussion feeling like my curiosity was a good thing and that life isn't so cut and dried as some religious folks would have you believe.

There's no question that I was incredibly fortunate to have a parent to whom I could bring these questions about my faith and not feel judged, but there was one issue I had questions about that I did not feel comfortable bringing to any adult in my life, including my mother. Perhaps I sensed that this issue was too edgy to breach with any elder, even in the context of an innocent, good faith dialogue with a young person who's just trying to learn what's right. Perhaps the connotations surrounding it that I'd picked up on let me know, implicitly, that there was no vagueness to this one, no argument to be made in favor of a gray area or change in rule. This issue was, to use the dehumanizingly clinical term favored by the conservative church both then and now (and thus the term that I would have used at the time), "homosexuality."

Whether it was because I grew up in a town located just a little over an hour's drive from San Francisco that had its own visibly out LGBTQ+ population or because of the relatively open-minded way my parents approached the world, I was never totally taken with the idea that being gay was sinful. The disgust that the wider church community of which I was a part seemed to feel toward anyone who wasn't straight was never something that I myself felt organically. That's not to say I didn't judge it as wrong or weird, but I didn't get why it was so evil. Other sins made sense, inherently. Murder, theft, adultery—those all hurt people in demonstrable ways. And worshipping idols and cursing? Well, I guess those somehow hurt God. When it came to homosexuality, though, I saw neither malice nor harm.

To be clear, I'm owed no compliments here. On the contrary, I myself owe many apologies. Just because I didn't get why I was supposed to see being gay as sinful doesn't mean I didn't agree to take a stand against it, as I was told to do. I might not have felt deep down that being gay was wrong, but I told people that being gay was wrong. Just like I told them Jesus was the only path to heaven, even when I couldn't explain it for myself. Just like I joined my fellow churchgoers in speaking disparagingly of my public high school teachers who refused to teach creationism as a legitimate theory, even though it was clear to me by then that evolution had a major part to play in how we all got here.

The point is, taking all of these stories into consideration, it's clear to me now that very little of what I felt I needed to profess or abide by as a Christian actually made sense to me in the moment—that I never fully understood the logic of the theology I'd been handed. In short, I had my doubts. But—and this is a big "but" for evangelicals—none of it needed to make sense. And not only did nothing of what I was being taught in church need to make sense, it almost wasn't supposed to.

There's a verse in the New Testament, in Paul's first letter to the Corinthians, that says, by one translation, "The wisdom of the world is foolishness in God's sight." In the same letter, Paul also writes, "the Lord knows the reasonings of the wise, that they are useless." If you flip back to the Old Testament, the prophet Jeremiah proclaimed that "the heart is deceitful above all things, and desperately sick." And even more harshly, per Jeremiah: "All mankind is stupid, devoid of knowledge."

Basically, what we have here is a lot of scripture—scripture I frequently heard quoted in church services and youth group meetings alike—detailing how imbecilic and evil humans are. And how, because of our naturally muddled mental state, all of the things we think are right about the world are idiotic from God's perspective. Combine all that with verses like Isaiah 55:8 ("'For My thoughts are not your thoughts, nor are your ways My ways,' declares the Lord."), Job 11:7 ("Can you discover the depths of God? Can you discover the limits of the Almighty?"), and, moving up to the New Testament again, Romans 11:33 ("How unsearchable are His judgments and unfathomable His ways!"), and you start to get an idea of how far evangelicals can take the idea that God moves in mysterious ways.

This is what I grew up with—this conviction that whenever something I was being taught in church felt wrong or unreasonable, it was because I was incapable of understanding it. All of the scripture, all of the theology, all of the tradition was right in one way or another. There was no question about that. To claim otherwise would be arrogance. To think that I knew better than God, who was all knowing and loved everyone perfectly and had existed before time and would continue to exist for eternity, was not an option. The only choice was to accept the fact that if a tenet felt unreasonable, it was some shortcoming of my own that kept me from being able to fully grasp the truth.

Did it seem illogical that even apparently good people would go to hell if they didn't ask Jesus to come into their hearts? Well, logic was not an authority for me. Did it feel amiss, in my gut, that people's natural attractions were an abomination to the God who created them? It didn't matter. My intuition was not—could not—be an authority. Only God's word was authority. And how was God's word delivered? Through the church; through anyone working for the church. Thus, if I heard it from a church-based source, whether it made sense to me was irrelevant. I would, quite literally, get a chance to understand when I was dead.

I accepted this self-denying deal without even really thinking about it. In part it was because the church had me from birth, so I never had the chance to get to an age of self-awareness before this worldview became my norm. Also, as I mentioned before, even when the abstract-thinking powers of my frontal lobe finally kicked in during adolescence, the risk of rejecting the religion and losing everything my young life revolved around was too great to fathom.

So, I stuck around through the anxiety-inducing summer camp dramas. I stuck around through hearing that Catholics aren't Christians, even though I was pretty sure they still believed that Jesus died and rose again for their sins. I stuck around through fundamentalist interpretations of Genesis even though people had obviously found dinosaur bones in the ground. I even stuck around, I am most ashamed to say, through an undying insistence that being gay was both a choice and a sin, even though I knew something about that was off. But still, I stuck around.

Looking back now, I wonder how many people I could have had more pleasant relationships with if I had been more resolute about renouncing, even just to myself, the misleading messages being pushed on me? How much less anxiety would I have had? How much more present and supportive I could have been, if I hadn't been taught to disregard what was demonstrably true? "What if" is a dangerous trail to trace, but when I look back, I wonder how much earlier I could have started getting out if I had given more credence to my doubts...if I had taken more of a chance on my intuition...if I had trusted better my own reasonably capable mind.

I'm not mad at myself, exactly. I know I was doing what most people under the same circumstances might have done, and I forgive myself for it—or at least I'm trying to. Plus, the truth is that I was the victim of some serious manipulation at the hands of people who had themselves been manipulated in the most recent iteration of a generational cycle that goes back a very long way. At the same time, I grieve my lack of confidence and my susceptibility to nonsense.

Yet even in the midst of that grief, as I step back to take a broader view of my journey through and out of Christianity, I can see how even just noticing the suspicions I had about my faith when I was young, small and unwelcome as they were at the time, prepared me to be that much more open-minded later in life, and then even a little more open-minded after that. And, thanks in large part to my not-nearly-as-conservative-as-it-could've-been home life and the heavily pluralistic local culture that surrounded me as I grew up, I do think that I paid just enough attention to my own misgivings about the theology I was being taught that I didn't suffocate those doubts completely. For these things I am immensely grateful.

On top of everything, as much as there is to forgive my younger self for, she is also the one who took a chance, who took the first step, unsteady as it was, and so she is due the biggest thank you of all.

Now, dear reader, I turn it over to you. What doubts do you have that you can pay a little more attention to? Maybe you don't have any, and that's perfectly fine too. But if you do, I encourage you: concede their presence. Don't sweep them under the rug. Sit with them; figure out what they're saying. And—this is important—don't argue with them. We know all the responses, we evangelicals. We have our own special version of reason—our supposedly cutting, theoretically Bible-based retorts to just about anything anyone could throw at us in heated debate. We are well trained, and we turn these weapons against our true selves daily.

As you consider taking this step, it's also important to keep in mind that doubt expresses itself to individuals in different forms. Perhaps your doubt speaks to you as that proverbially still, small voice, otherwise known as a conscience, and you kind of hear it in your head. Perhaps your doubt is more like a feeling somewhere in your body, alerting you to a misalignment between what you're being told and what seems more fundamentally true. Or maybe doubt appears to you through your mind's eye as a vision or image, like a warning light on a car's dashboard. Whatever your mode of perception—and if you're not quite sure which you're working with, take some time to learn—don't ignore the message. You don't need to act on it, but please acknowledge it.

What I'm really asking you to do in this first step is stop. Stop going through the motions of arguing yourself back into compliance. Stop reciting the apologetics of Christian philosophers that you know so well, that were given to you to keep the important questions at bay. Just let the hesitations speak. Try not to dismiss your doubt as an understandable but silly pop-up of the inevitably limited human mind. Keep the unanswered inquiries beside you, even if the path you walk continues to be within the fold.

I'm not saying it will be easy to sit with your doubts as if they're worthy of your time, but this is the work that needs to be done if we're to have a chance at living a life that's aligned with our own deepest convictions. We are retraining ourselves here. And if there's anything the church taught me that actually turns out to be true, it's that sooner is better than later when it comes to conditioning the mind.

The sooner you ask yourself "What if I'm not the one who's wrong?" when you feel that stirring of skepticism in reaction to a church teaching, the sooner you'll start the journey toward freedom. The sooner you recognize that you might be going along with church teachings against your own best judgment only because of fear or shame, as I did when I so quickly accepted the idea that I was responsible for everyone's souls, the sooner you'll have a starting point from which to move forward on your quest for true salvation.

I went back and forth over the years in my own relationship with my doubts. At best, I felt safe to express them and found ways to make compromises in logic that allowed me to continue living my faith in relative comfort—until the next hesitation appeared, of course. At worst, I believed the world was facing impending doom and it was crucial that I ignore all my uncertainties lest I fail at the task of being a good Christian and face the disappointment of God. The weight of the consequences varied, but in either case I was usually coaxed into a denial of my heart and mind.

Can you identify when you are doing, or being asked to do, the same? Can you detect the gentlest of tugs on your soul or conscience or whatever you want to call it when the church is telling you to stand here but some part of you knows you'd be much more comfortable over there? I hope so. I hope you don't write your instincts off as foolishness. They might not be perfect, but they are not corrupt. You are good, despite any message to the contrary that you've been told to believe about yourself. You've got what it takes to be decent in this world. And if there's ever a disconnect between what your heart is telling you and the church's teachings, I hope you stay open to the possibility that you're not the one who's wrong.

STEP 2
GET ANGRY WITH GOD

"Why" was my favorite word as a child. As soon as I was old enough to understand what it meant, I began using it against my parents daily. Whenever they asked me to put away my toys, my first response was, "Why?" Whenever they implored me to be nicer to my sister, I retorted, "Why?" Even if they were just letting me know what was going to happen next, like if we needed to go to the grocery store to get ingredients for dinner, I insisted on knowing why. And, to what I'm sure was their great frustration, one answer was rarely sufficient. Whether they gave me a patiently constructed, truthful explanation or came back with a good old-fashioned "Because I said so," I usually couldn't help but continue to push against the situation even harder: "But *why*?"

Clearly, the actual truth was not all that I was looking for. Sometimes I wanted to stall as much as possible before beginning an inevitable and unpleasant chore; sometimes I was feeling particularly pugnacious. Ultimately, though, what I always enjoyed was the feeling of engaging with another person in a cerebral tennis match. Not that my five-year-old "Why?" was a particularly cutting inquiry, but it was an age-appropriate manifestation of this aspect of my personality: a craving to conscript other folks in my own analytical excavation of the world's mysteries, including my inclination to tear down whatever ideas didn't seem right or fair from my point of view.

I'll be the first to admit that this isn't always the most charming quality, especially when used in bad faith or with the goal of dismantling another person's worldview so I could recruit them to my own. But it was a big part of why I felt even the slightest bit comfortable asking my mother about those aspects of our church's theology that didn't quite make sense to me, like the commitment to creationism or the bitter disdain for the Catholic faith. I liked pressing myself and others to the very edges of "Why?" even if the others weren't particularly keen on going there themselves.

That said, this impulse also had its limits. In regard to religion, I asked "Why?" about a lot of things the church told me to believe, but I never asked "Why?" about the church itself. I wondered how to interpret certain verses, but not whether the Bible as whole was heaven-sent. I questioned what God might want from us—did He really need us to convert everyone in our path? Did He really hate gay people that much?—but it never crossed my mind that He might not exist at all.

When it came down to it, my "why's" about the church were a decidedly intellectual exercise. They didn't infiltrate my heart, the power station fueling my religious devotion, where all of my love for the Lord and my unquestioning belief in His goodness resided. I had my uncertainties about particular details, but my faith in the ultimate truth of Christianity was never under interrogation.

There's no question that paying attention to my doubts was an important first step for me, and would have gone a long way in saving me from a life of totally mindless obedience to the church even if it were all I ever did, but it was still only one small movement forward on my journey away from the belief system in which I was raised. I could have stayed in that spot forever, just one stride away from fundamentalism, debating theological minutiae with fellow believers and thinking that I was one of those special Christians who really had considered everything. If I was ever going to gain some purchase on my path and have a real shot at breaking free from the church's gravitational pull, though, I needed the opportunity to go beyond the questioning of abstract ideas and grapple with some truly personal dilemmas.

What I needed, it turns out, was to get angry. I mean really, genuinely angry. The kind of anger that transcends your run-of-the-mill frustration. The kind you feel when you know you are in the right and your dignity is on the line and it can't be just a matter of turning the other cheek. The kind of anger that demands a reckoning. I needed to experience what it felt like to be outraged at God.

Of course, this kind of anger doesn't come out of nowhere. It requires a catalyst. Something dreadful that happens to you that's beyond your fault or control. For me, that situation was the Break-Up. You know the Break-Up, right? That one death of a relationship that is seared in your memory because it left you wondering if you'd ever be happy again; the one where you learn that it's called a broken heart because your insides physically hurt. The one that, you were sure, no matter how young you were, signaled the end of your love life forever.

Mine happened when I was twenty-five, but we have to go back a few years before that to understand why the end of this particular relationship, which was technically only a couple of months long, took the wind out of me the way that it did, and how it opened up what turned out to be an insurmountable chasm between me and the Lord.

FROM THE MOMENT puberty kicked in, having a romantic partner was one of my highest priorities and most persistent concerns, second only to obeying God's word and spreading the good news of Jesus around the world. Indeed, it was one of the church's highest priorities, too—one of the things that we God-fearing folks were called to do with our lives: get married, then be fruitful and multiply. The general consensus in our little subculture seemed to be that adult life didn't really start until you tied the knot.

This obsession with monogamous heterosexual romance is not unique to American evangelical Christianity, of course. Everything I consumed outside of the church context—books, movies, TV shows, advertisements—backed up this idea that true fulfillment, the highest form of happiness, came from having a significant other of the opposite sex who was madly in love with you. Considering the church world and the secular world had basically the same stance on the subject, it's no wonder I bought so fully into the idea that my life would not be complete without a guy.

The idea took up such a significant amount of real estate in my mind that I, like the God-fearing girl that I was, started praying for a boyfriend when I was in seventh grade. Every night before I fell asleep—and I do mean every night—surrounded by pictures of impossibly handsome leading men that I'd cut out from magazines and taped across every inch of my bedroom walls, I'd take a few moments to let the Lord know all that I was thankful for and all that I wanted from

Him. At the top of my list of requests was always a romantic partner. Someone to share my thoughts with who was more than a friend. Someone to snuggle and hug and hold hands with. Someone to confirm for myself and the world that I was attractive to and wanted by the half of the population that was supposed to be attracted to and want me.

In college, my petition shifted from "boyfriend" to "husband." I was also starting to get a little worried. Other than a month-long and very awkward relationship with a co-worker the summer after I graduated from high school, my daily pleading for someone to couple up with was going unanswered. No one asked me to prom. No one ever asked me out, period. If I was going to be married by twenty-five as I'd planned (in Christian circles, a respectable age to make this life-long commitment), something was going to have to change, and soon.

It wasn't just that I was anxious to get going on the prescribed timeline for my life, though. I was also growing troublingly insecure about my worth, which, as a young woman, was tied to my looks with a knot so taut and old that the possibility of separating the two never even crossed my mind. Not having any young men show interest in me, especially at a Christian college, was more than disappointing; I was growing seriously concerned that I was fundamentally undesirable inside and out.

It was during this state of slow-growing mental distress at the thought of my perpetual singleness that I met Chris (or so I'll call him for the sake of this story). He appeared at my dorm room door a couple of months before the end of my sophomore year, asking my roommate if he could copy her notes from a class they were both taking.

Now, our school was quite small—barely more than a thousand students in total—so it was rare to make it through two whole years without at least knowing the names of most of your fellow students. Nevertheless, I hadn't heard of Chris before, let alone seen him. Perhaps the fact that he'd been so elusive was part of the charm, but I swear I saw a literal twinkle in his eye when my roommate introduced us to each other. I liked him immediately, and I was pretty sure he found me interesting, too.

As it turns out, I was right. It wasn't long before he started coming back by my room just to chat. Then, we began having meals together in the cafeteria and going for hikes in the hills behind campus on the weekends. Eventually, we were watching movies together in my building's lounge and napping side by side on my narrow school-issued twin bed.

I was thrilled. Finally, here was a guy I was really, truly attracted to—not just because he was cute, but because we laughed together, and he was smart and interested in the world and seemed like a little bit of a rebel—who was going out of his way to show me that he was also attracted to me.

Well, mostly. There was one gesture I was waiting for—that I'd been waiting for long before I met Chris—that didn't happen. He never asked me out on a real date. Despite the snuggling and the late-night studying and Saturday morning hikes, just the two of us, our relationship existed in a limbo of non-definition, clearly more than a friendship but not involving any commitment, either. What we had, in fact, was a classic Christian kid fling (and I'm using the word "fling" here generously): about six weeks of some sexually charged one-on-one time that went no further in terms of physical intimacy than the occasional spooning when no one else was around and never involved an honest conversation about what was going on between us.

I was tempted to be upset about it—I certainly wanted for things between us to progress and for me to be his girlfriend

—but I knew what the barrier was. He was about to graduate and backpack around Europe with a friend from school for a couple of months before deciding what to do with the rest of his life. I, on the other hand, still had two more years of college left. There was really no point in making things official. At least, I gathered that's what Chris was thinking. And I understood. As desperate as I was to be ensconced in a serious relationship, there was no denying that the timing of our flirtation was not conducive to a long-term commitment.

Our goodbye at the end of the semester was brief. We hugged, then he hopped in his friend's car to head to the airport. As I waved him off, I tried to focus on the positive. What had transpired between us wasn't quite the answer to prayer that I'd been looking for, but it did give me encouragement that I wasn't totally repellant to the opposite sex. It also gave me faith. I took Chris's presence in my life as a sign from God that He was indeed listening and working on the husband thing behind the scenes. Perhaps this small, innocent dalliance was like a piece of manna, meant to tide me over until I reached the promised land and the real feast began. I didn't feel satisfied, but I was grateful.

UNFORTUNATELY, the gratitude I felt for the time I was able to spend with Chris and the pleasure his attention brought me only lasted so long. By the time I returned to campus the next fall, my preoccupation with being coupled was back in full force. All through the rest of my time in college and even after I moved back to my hometown once I was done with school, I was constantly on the lookout for the man I was meant to be with—the man I was sure God had waiting for me just as I was waiting, and praying, for him. I had plenty of crushes—

on coworkers, on guys I knew from high school, on one neighbor who was so obviously bad news, but he was too cute and I was too naïve to notice. But no one ever reciprocated my interest like Chris did.

The worst times were when I was at church, surrounded by people with whom I was supposedly sharing the same blessed path. I looked around at the folks there who were my age and it seemed like every last one of them had a significant other. As far as I could tell, they were all either married or headed straight toward it, and spending time with them each week only reminded me of what I knew I was meant to have —what I was taught I could expect to be given by God—yet could not find. I had to wonder, what were they doing right that I wasn't? I might have been born with a natural inclination to question the Christian tenets that tested the edges of my credulity, but there was no question in my mind that I was not meant to be alone.

What I did continue to question, however, thanks to the incredibly narrow norms by which I was surrounded, was my own worthiness. My own beauty. My own likeability. Now and then, when it felt safe to do so, I would interrogate people I trusted—my mother, and a couple of particularly close friends—about why I wasn't appealing to guys. Was I ugly? Was I annoying? Of course, I framed the questions just like that, in self-pitying ways, so their responses were always insistent on my prettiness and charm and intelligence, as if I'd been fishing for reassurance. Maybe a part of me had, but I also did really want to know what I could do differently, and I never got a straight answer.

I asked God these things, too, though talking with Him was more like wondering out loud. Knowing that He wasn't usually one to respond with an immediate, audible remark, I voiced my desperate queries about where I'd gone wrong into the silence around me late at night and then kept my eyes open for His answers in the following days. My experience was that He communicated in indirect ways, through signs and happenstance and seemingly random notions, so I watched for clues about what I could do to up the chances of meeting a good Christian man who would want to spend the rest of his life with me.

One day, after a few hours spent typing numbers into a spreadsheet for the entry-level job I'd taken right out of college, I had an idea. The memory of a friend's experience with an international Christian missionary organization popped into my head. I'd been intrigued by her stories of spending six months in another country studying the Bible and doing community service, and it led me to thinking that maybe I wasn't meeting anyone because I hadn't fully aligned myself with God's will for my life. Maybe working in a windowless room for a company that had nothing to do with what I'd just spent four years and a lot of money studying was not the destiny God had in store for me, and He was waiting until I stepped into something I was truly passionate about before bringing me the partner He'd ordained.

I started doing some research. I discovered that the organization my friend had worked with had a base in New Zealand that offered a six-month missionary training course with an outdoor adventure theme, which meant that your missionary education came with some camping, rock climbing, and kayaking on the side. Having just seen the movie *Whale Rider*, I'd recently become obsessed with New Zealand, so I took my discovery of this option as a sign that I was headed in the right direction. I sent in my application, got accepted, gathered together a few thousand dollars of other people's money, and, in the fall of 2004, left the U.S. to see what God had in store for me on the other side of the world.

HOW TO LEAVE THE CHURCH

The story of my time training and working as a missionary with that organization is a long one on its own, full of both trauma and joy, and one day I might tell it in depth. For the purposes of this narrative, though, I want to focus on just one thing I learned while I was there.

The entire group at the training school, which included around thirty of us students and a handful of volunteer staff, spent the first three months of our program attending lectures and working on service projects with the local community on the North Island of New Zealand before then breaking into smaller groups to evangelize in entirely different countries for another two or three months. The lectures were on topics ranging from specific books of the Bible to spiritual warfare to best practices for proselytizing. Sometimes the base staff would be the ones teaching, and sometimes they'd bring in speakers from outside. In either case, we would usually spend a full work week, Monday through Friday, on each subject, with the lectures taking up at least a couple of hours on each of those days.

Despite the abundance of religious teachings—and the extensive notes we were all compelled to take—there's very little I remember from those classes. Except for the week we focused on relationships. Yes, we spent an entire week learning about God's will for us when it came to romantic couplings, and during that week, whoever happened to be giving the lectures shared this ringing adage: "Be the one before you find the one."

I don't know if the speaker made it up or borrowed it from someone else, but the phrase really struck me, and stuck with me. As concerned as ever about my prospects for marriage, or lack thereof, something inside of me clicked when I heard it. It felt like God was speaking right to me. Was this the answer I'd been praying for? Is this why nothing ever worked out with all the young men I'd liked before? Maybe I was too focused on charming them and needed to work more on improving myself. Maybe I needed to let go of the begging for a husband, reallocate that energy toward preparing myself to be the best partner I could be, and trust God that if I was faithful, the man of my dreams would come.

This idea was in the forefront of my mind when I returned to California after half a year spent overseas. Once I unpacked, found a new job, and bought another car (I'd sold my previous one to help pay for the missionary school), I sat in my old room in my parents' house and made a commitment to taking responsibility for my side of the equation when it came to my romantic life. I was going to be the one so I could find the one.

I started drawing and painting in my free time. I read more, and wrote more too. I picked up the guitar I'd been neglecting since before I left for the other side of the world. When I wasn't at work or helping out with the youth group at the church I grew up in, I spent a lot of time in my bedroom, alone, much of it talking to God. In the past I would have done so feeling sorry for myself; there would have been no solitude for me without loneliness. But I'd been invigorated by what I'd heard when I was in New Zealand. I was feeling powerful. I was learning to like hanging out with myself.

After a number of months spent investing in this practice of self-love, of embracing my life as it was and finding meaning in a routine of work and service and play, another notion occurred to me. Now, I'd been on a roll when it came to identifying signs from God and adjusting my trajectory accordingly. The missionary school had worked out quite well in that regard, and I was on the lookout for the next burning bush in the form of another random idea or impromptu scheme to light my way as I did my best to follow God's plan for my life. But this notion—this one was a little suspect. I couldn't tell if it was actually God trying to speak to me or just my old attachments and insecurities showing up to tempt me into straying from the Lord.

The notion was this: I started to think about Chris.

At first it was just a little flash of curiosity. His name popped into my head, I spent a minute wondering what he'd been up to over the last couple of years, and I went on with my day. Then, thoughts of him began to visit more frequently, and for longer stretches of time. The experience wasn't necessarily pleasant. On the contrary, having finally broken free from my habit of perpetually pining for romance thanks to all the time and energy I'd spent focusing on myself since returning to the States, I was almost annoyed. I did not fancy my brain space being taken up by images of a man who had decided not to pursue me. I was eager to keep working on myself so that I would be at my best when God brought me and my future husband together.

Even so, I couldn't help wondering if Chris had come to mind for a reason. I knew—well, I was fairly certain—that I no longer had any interest in him. Sure, I'd thought about him now and then in the months following our time together. We'd exchanged a few emails after he left for Europe, and we even saw each other once more in person when he came back to campus to watch a friend graduate the following May. But with each interaction, I could sense the undertones of flirtation fading further and further away. By the time I myself graduated, the emails had stopped, and we lost touch completely.

Given all that, when his name began appearing in my brain out of nowhere, it didn't feel like I was choosing to think about him. Honestly, I might have preferred to never think about him again. But being the earnest disciple that I was, I had to ask if God was trying to tell me something. Was He nudging me to reach out to Chris, just to say hello and see if he was well? Was I being tapped to fulfill a divine mission by sending an encouraging message to an old friend? Or perhaps my motives were indeed suspect. What if there was a part of my subconscious that still liked him and hoped that something romantic could happen between us, and that's why I was thinking about contacting him?

I went back and forth with these questions for a few weeks, emphatic about considering the circumstances thoroughly. I prayed for wisdom and waited for more information, but it never came. What did come was an awareness that my fretting over the situation was not sustainable. I was starting to feel silly spending so much time deciding whether to say hello to a guy I barely knew and hadn't spoken to in nearly three years.

I had to make a choice: forget about Chris once and for all, or send him an email. Of course, the first option was easier said than done—the whole reason I found myself in this dilemma was the fact that I couldn't forget about him. On top of that, to move on without reaching out was to risk ignoring God's will. Then there was the second option, which was risky in its own way. Chris might find my check-in intrusive and tell me to leave him alone for good. Such a rejection had the potential to push me back into the realm of self-pity about my lack of luck with the opposite sex, a realm I'd managed to claw my way out of over the last six months.

In the end, I decided that I feared the regret of missing out on what the Lord might have in store for me more than I feared whatever answer I might get from a mortal man, so I wrote and sent the email. Strangely enough, once I entrusted my communication to the intangible void that is cyberspace, using the years-old email address I had for him (that I wasn't entirely sure he even checked anymore), the thought of Chris slipped quietly from my mind. The minute I no longer felt like I was carrying around an unfulfilled responsibility—once I could say to myself that I did my best to follow through on what I thought God might be asking me to do—I actually did forget about him.

Until he wrote me back.

Three days after I sent my email, I logged in to my account and discovered a message from Chris in my inbox, bold and ready to be opened. When I clicked on it, a multi-paragraph letter appeared, so long it couldn't all fit on the desktop monitor's screen. I inhaled sharply when I saw it, simultaneously terrified and excited about what the many words might say.

After some standard opening salutations, the dispatch became quite detailed, revealing that Chris too had been on a journey of self-actualization since we last talked. He had reconnected with Jesus and was intensely involved in a church down in Orange County, where he now lived. His email also made it clear that he was happy to hear from me, and wanted to know more about what I was up to.

Talk about a sign. As far as I was concerned, this was a buzzing neon billboard shining down from the heavens to let me know that I had made the right decision when I reached out. It was, in fact, the first of many signs regarding me and Chris that were to come in the months that followed—signs that, like trail markers along an unfamiliar route I'd decided to hike on a whim and without a map, brought relief and increasing confidence every time I saw them. Signs I thought I could trust because they felt so damn authoritative. Signs that left me no choice but to believe that I was on the right track, following a path created just for me by a loving God who deemed me ready—finally!—to receive the gift that I'd been praying for since I was thirteen years old.

At first, the guideposts were far apart and not always obvious. After I wrote Chris back with more details about my life, we began a regular correspondence that grew more eager with each passing week. Eventually we were texting with each other nearly every day and talking on the phone for hours on the weekends. Over the course of these conversations, little things were said—mentions of the dreams we had for our own lives, offhand comments about our thoughts on God and other theological musings—that revealed bit by bit just how much we had in common. Of course, we'd had some things in common back in college, too, and nothing of lasting significance came from it, so I was wary of reading too much into these shared interests. Still, it was nice to have someone to connect with. I was enjoying our renewed friendship and trying hard to keep myself from expecting anything more than that.

Then, after a couple of months, the signs started getting bigger and brighter, and my caution started to feel more like a lack of faith than wisdom. First, there was the issue of our geography. Part of what made it easy for me to stay relatively detached as Chris and I were getting reacquainted was the fact that we were doing so nearly four hundred miles away from each other. I couldn't see him in person; I couldn't touch him. The distance was a natural barrier. But as it turned out, it was going to be short-lived. During one of our hours-long phone calls, it came out that both he and I had applied for grad school in Southern California that coming September—he to a PhD program not far from where he lived in Orange County, and I to a master's program at a seminary in Pasadena, just east of L.A. Assuming we both got in and accepted our spots (which we did, not long after the subject of our plans came up), it meant that we'd be within an hour's drive of each other in less than six months.

This was a coincidence I couldn't force myself to interpret as chance. Not as a trusting follower of God. Forget the little similarities that kept us talking well into the evenings; like I said, those weren't so glaring as far as trail markers go. This fact, though—that we would soon be able to see each other in-person regularly and be pursuing our callings in the same way at the same time, basically side-by-side—read like a placard written in bold, capital letters: "YOU ARE GOING THE RIGHT WAY!" with an arrow pointing toward a future that Chris was definitely in.

The next big sign came when we decided to make plans to get together in person before the school year started and the inevitable deluge of coursework took over our lives. I don't remember who proposed the idea first, but we'd been talking about how badly we wanted to see each other face-to-face even before we'd each committed to our respective degree programs. Once our plans for the fall were set, one or the other of us figured out that there was going to be a week-long stretch at the end of August when we could actually make it happen. Chris would be spending most of the summer in Tijuana, helping to build houses for an organization his church regularly partnered with. Then, he was going to head up to the Pacific Northwest to visit his family over Labor Day weekend before returning to Southern California to get ready for school. In between those two commitments, he had seven days, and in those seven days, we decided, he was going to come spend some time with me and my family in my hometown.

I smiled to myself every time I thought of how things were coming together. Granted, just like when we first met in those last couple months of my sophomore year of college, our conversations deftly avoided any open inquiry about what was going on between us. I didn't know if Chris was seeing the signs, too—if he was thinking God might be bringing us together. If he was hoping we might be more than friends someday soon. But he did agree to buy a plane ticket to come up and visit me. And, he agreed to stay in my parents' house for a week to see a little bit of the place that made me who I was. I might not have had much experience with dating up to that point, but I was pretty sure these weren't the actions of a disinterested man.

Also not a sign of romantic disinterest? Driving from Mexico into California at the end of a long day to call someone from an American payphone just because you missed hearing their voice. We'd been forced to put our weekly conversations on hold when Chris moved down to Tijuana for the summer, what with international calling still being prohibitively expensive for most folks in 2006. I'd gotten used to our communication being temporarily confined to email and was not planning on having any interaction beyond that until he came back to the States for good at the end of the season. So, when I answered a call from a number I didn't recognize a few weeks after his departure, "Hey, it's Chris" were the last words I expected to hear come crackling over the faded line. He said he'd been so impatient to speak to me that he drove back across the border with a handful of quarters, hoping to catch me for just a few minutes before his change ran out.

We didn't talk for long, and I don't remember about what, but of course it wasn't the details of the conversation that mattered. What Chris had given me with that phone call, whether he was conscious of it or not, was the next big sign. And not just any sign—the exact one that I'd been waiting for: evidence that he was in it for more than friendship, that he too felt something special going on between us. Thanks to that call, when I picked him up from the airport outside of my hometown a few weeks later, I had nothing but faith that what we were going to build in our time together that week was what God had intended for us all along, even back when it seemed like we'd gone our separate ways for good.

Seven days later, my faith proved well-placed. I'd filled his visit to the brim with beach trips, hikes through the redwoods and over the hills that peeked out onto the bay, and small gatherings with friends whose approval Chris would ultimately need if he was going to be my significant other someday. Chris himself even suggested a spontaneous detour or two, including a valiant but ultimately unsuccessful attempt at solving a giant hay bale maze we discovered on the side of the road as we were driving to a beach a few miles north of town.

By our final night together, we were pretty exhausted. Chris proposed spending the evening in, just relaxing and talking, so we headed to the store to grab some snacks before returning to my parents' house and settling down in front of the TV in the living room. It was then, after my parents went to bed and the house was quiet, as we sat on the carpeted floor between the couch and the coffee table, sharing a pint of Ben and Jerry's, that he told me he thought he might want to marry me and asked if I would be his girlfriend.

Even as I write about that moment now, fifteen years later, I'm nearly speechless. How can I describe what I felt in that moment? After so many months of trying to stay patient as I watched our relationship germinate, wondering if we were growing what I hoped we were growing—after so many years spent begging God to bring me a boyfriend, then a husband, and working so hard to read the signs right—it was finally, actually happening. There was a thrill, and relief, and maybe even a little disbelief. Given how long I'd been waiting for it, the moment was kind of surreal.

There was also surprise—not that Chris wanted something more than friendship, but that he'd gone so far as to bring up marriage. Although that was my ultimate goal, I hadn't expected things to get that serious that fast. He and I certainly hadn't talked about getting hitched, to each other or anyone else. But I was happy to dare to be so hopeful if he was, so I said "Yes," and we officially became a couple.

Before I started this story, I mentioned that my relationship with Chris was technically only a couple of months long. Indeed, though I moved down to Pasadena jittery with pride over finally being partnered up, secretly relishing every chance I had to say, "my boyfriend," each utterance of the phrase like the quick flash of a passport confirming I was worthy to live in the land of the loved, that cherished citizenship was soon—and surprisingly—stripped away.

I hadn't expected things to be perfect once we were both down in Southern California. I knew we would each be seriously busy with our classes—which we were—and that it would be annoying to have to drive no less than an hour each way to see each other on the weekends, which it was. But Chris had said that he might want to marry me, and in my mind that meant that he had a vision for us that extended far beyond all of those immediate inconveniences. I thought that building a long-term relationship with me was now among his highest priorities. And I definitely thought, because it never occurred to me not to assume it, that he was attracted to me. He'd certainly seemed proud to introduce me to his friends the first time I drove down to visit him in Orange County.

Given all that, I wasn't particularly concerned when, about two weeks after I'd finished moving into my new apartment in Pasadena, Chris quietly pulled his hand away from mine for no apparent reason as we were walking back to my place from a party one warm Saturday night.

Or, more accurately, I chose not to let myself grow too concerned. In truth, his action, subtle as it must have seemed to any onlookers, stood out to me. It was the first time I'd felt any semblance of rejection from him since I'd said hello out of nowhere ten months prior, and it succeeded in igniting a small flame of misgiving in my heart that I knew was in danger of growing into a full-blown blaze of anxiety if I didn't keep it in check. Were that to happen—were my deepest fears and insecurities about my lovability to take over—I suspected I would start acting in a way that came off as desperate. I would become the "crazy" girlfriend, no matter the legitimacy of my worries, which would push Chris away even further. I couldn't let that happen.

I also wanted to keep trusting God. After all, He'd brought me this far. I hadn't had to force anything or pretend to be someone I wasn't in order to get Chris to like me. All I did was show up, wait for the signs, and keep going in the direction they were pointing, and it had led me to a relationship that was more than I'd hoped for. Deep down, I was confident that this thing between me and Chris was God's will. I was sure it was divinely ordained. When I thought about that, I knew I had to believe that whatever the reason Chris had slipped his hand out of mine as we walked through the city on that warm September night, it could not be anything worth stressing out over. I chose to have faith, to let it go. And, in fact, I did succeed in putting it from my mind, until the next weekend, when Chris brought it up unprompted.

It was my turn to travel to where he was, so I met him at his church on Sunday morning and then we drove separately to get a bite to eat nearer to his school. After lunch, we went back to his campus apartment, and as I sat on the couch waiting for him to get settled in and join me, he came out from his bedroom and asked if I'd noticed how he didn't want to hold my hand after the party the previous weekend.

"Yeah," I said, that smothered ember of unease now threatening once again to reignite inside me.

He went on to say that it had felt weird all of a sudden, holding my hand. He couldn't explain what the issue was, but he'd been talking with a friend from church about it ever since it happened. Together, they'd come to the conclusion that it would be best if he and I spent some time completely apart from each other so he could sort through his feelings—specifically, he wanted two weeks with no communication.

I had no response. Clearly, he had thought this through in detail without me. On top of that, the issue seemed more serious than I'd imagined since he was willing to go two whole weeks without talking or texting. But he wouldn't explain things any further, and he'd devised a strategy to deal with it—whatever it was—without my help or input. Without even letting me know what was going on until things were already decided. As far as I could see, my only choices were to push back against his sequestering approach, which risked deepening the conflict, or go along with it. Since I was doing my best to let God's plan unfold as it was supposed to, and I'd long ago been indoctrinated into the idea that a righteous woman's greatest gift to her husband is her full support, I acquiesced and left.

I passed the days that followed trying to focus on schoolwork, but mostly I just prayed a lot. Even more than worried, I was confused. Had I done something to upset him? Was he struggling with an issue from his past that had nothing to do with me? I didn't know how to pray for him, let alone us, so I just kept asking God to guide him through whatever resistance he was feeling about me or our relationship.

I myself was still completely convinced that we were each other's destiny, and that faith, coupled with my knowledge of how devout a believer Chris had become, helped sustain me through those strange, silent fourteen days. The experience was far from easy, but I had confidence that we would make it to the other side. I even got to the point where I was thankful for the challenge, believing that God would use it to make us stronger as a couple in the end.

As it happened, two weeks from the day Chris said he wanted to take a break was a weekend we'd already planned to spend in Tijuana. An opportunity to help build a house for a family in need had come up well before the hand-holding incident, and he'd invited me to come along. Strange as it would be to regroup by spending two hours in a car together and then jumping right into manual labor, I felt optimistic about the trip. I saw it as an opportunity to demonstrate how excited I was to be a part of his life and his interests. I thought that if I was present as my best, most agreeable and enthusiastic self, I could remind him of how he'd felt about me before things got weird in his mind.

I was also delighted to see this part of his life in person. He seemed relaxed and happy there in his element. We visited the home he had stayed in over the summer. He took me to his favorite taco spot, and I heard him converse at length in Spanish—one of his great loves—for the first time. I watched him glow with sweat and purpose as he worked to create the frame of a house from what had once been just a pile of lumber and a pouch full of nails. And during that construction session, as Chris was hammering away and laughing with a friend under the bright sun and I could feel the joy radiating off him—that's when I realized I loved him.

I kept the feeling to myself, secreting it away in my heart until the time was right to share it, like I'd found the perfect Christmas present for him, but it was still only July. After all, we had yet to broach the subject of his strange feeling about holding my hand, and I still didn't know how the last two weeks of no contact had been for him. Even without that conversation, though, I was feeling good about how the weekend was going. He hadn't pushed me away or seemed troubled, and I was sure that my private moment of revelation about how I truly felt toward him was yet another sign from God that we were still on the right path. By the time the next morning came around and we were on the road back home, my confidence in our destiny was more or less restored.

The line to cross the border back into California was long and slow. As we sat idling and hoping the car wouldn't overheat, looking out over the acres of dry dirt and yellowing grass that surrounded us, I thought of the night that summer when Chris wanted to speak to me so bad that he drove this very route to get to a phone he could use, not sure if I'd even answer when he called. I imagined the wait time for getting back into the States was a lot shorter on a weekday evening.

I was in the middle of quietly enjoying this memory when Chris spoke up. He started talking about cutting losses—at least, that's what I surmised after a few minutes of him describing a book (or perhaps an article; this detail is lost to me now) he'd recently read. He pointed to the other side of the road, empty compared to the jam we were in, and said that at a certain point, no matter how long we'd been patiently waiting for the creeping caravan of cars to get us to our planned destination, it would make more sense to pull out onto the open median, cross over to the southbound lanes, and head back in the direction we'd just come from.

Now, a person less naïve than I—a person whose whole understanding of God's vision for her life wasn't dependent on the ongoing success of this particular relationship—might have guessed right then and there that Chris was trying, however insufficiently, to communicate how he was feeling about our coupling. But he provided no context, and he didn't say anything else after he finished describing his illicit U-turn fantasy. Thanks to his reticence to be forthcoming and my righteous commitment to optimism, I didn't understand what he was getting at. Even if there was a part of me that did, it was successfully muffled by my stubborn faith that a period of solo reflection and a weekend spent doing what he loved had brought Chris back to a sense of comfort and purpose with me.

We made it across the border eventually, no U-turn necessary. Once we got through the checkpoint, the road was clear and the driving smooth. Exhausted from the whirlwind, work-filled weekend, we weren't talking much, just watching the rain-starved landscape spread out before us like the backdrop of a Western movie set. Personally, I found it comforting to just sit in silence and not feel the need to talk just for the sake of saying something out loud. I assumed Chris was enjoying the shared stillness, too, and that it would last us until we got home.

It wasn't until Chris started talking again, when we were halfway between Tijuana and Orange County, that I realized his quiet was not due to an absence of anything to say but a hesitance to utter the words he knew would break more than silence. We had just shy of an hour left in our drive—enough time to say what needed to be said and discuss it a bit, but not so long that we'd be stuck in mutual discomfort for what felt like forever—when he let me know, in the most matter-of-fact tone you can imagine, that we'd given this dating thing a fair shot, but it wasn't working out and it was time to split up.

I remember I was looking out the passenger side window. I remember feeling like I was in a dream. I could see the world around me passing by at freeway speeds, but none of it seemed real. I remember hearing myself ask him if I could still go to his church. He said I could do whatever I wanted. I remember I didn't cry.

I was still in shock when we pulled into the parking lot outside his apartment building. I moved my duffle bag stuffed with the previous day's sweaty, dust-covered clothes from his car to mine, and we hugged goodbye one last time. It was quick and muted—I still had no words. He didn't act sad, maybe because he wasn't.

Looking back, I can see that Chris had probably already moved on in his mind. In those two weeks we spent not communicating with each other, he'd made his decision. I, on the other hand, had spent those two weeks fighting back panic and choosing to be hopeful. I'd spent those two weeks assuming that it would take a lot more than a little discomfort for him to abandon all that he and I had been building over the last ten months.

None of it felt anywhere near real until I called my mom on my drive home and spoke out loud what he'd said to me. Finally, the tears came, and once they started, they didn't stop. I cried for two months straight. Sobbed. Wailed. Sometimes it was just alone in my apartment; sometimes it was to my mom over the phone. Mostly, though, it was to God.

Howling was the only language I had for the heartbreak I was experiencing—the heartbreak that was indeed a literal pain in my chest. I'd chosen a path of faith, bet everything I had on my belief that I'd read the signs right, allowed myself to be led by the Lord according to His timing despite every opportunity I had to try to rush things along out of my own anxiety and fear.

Now it was gone. All that I'd waited for. Everything I believed my life was going to be had been pulled out of my grateful arms in one unceremonious moment.

At first I blamed Chris. For weeks, my conviction that God intended for he and I to be together remained unwavering. As far as I was concerned, it was he who was standing in the way of the Lord's will—or walking away from it, to be more precise. I was convinced that he was acting out from a part of himself that he had yet to let God heal, a place of deep insecurity and shame. I believed he would rather lose me than have to let me all the way in, and I wanted to be the one to break through that hesitancy, to show him what a God-centered love could look like.

I tried to help him see it once, the root of his withdrawal. A few days after we broke up, I worked up the courage to call him and get more information about what had happened, why he was so sure that things between us had run their course. When I explained my theory that he was scared to be vulnerable, he chided me for playing armchair psychologist and told me that the situation wasn't a big deal and I needed to let it go. We'd only been going out for a couple of months, he said. I reminded him that he told me he might want to marry me. To this he had no response, beyond an admission that it was true. It was almost as if he'd forgotten that he said it.

After that conversation, it was clear to me that the only

thing that was going to salvage our relationship was divine intervention. So I continued to pray. I went for long walks around my neighborhood, squinting up at stucco-frosted midcentury apartment buildings baking in the Southern California sun, taking 90-degree turn after 90-degree turn around the gridded suburban streets that went nowhere in particular, listening for the voice of God, following my own personal concrete labyrinth.

As I walked, I thought about how the Lord had brought Chris and I back together once, and how I knew He could do it again. Why wouldn't He? I was faithful, I was obedient, and I'd been waiting for the gift of a partner for so, so long. I had to believe that no deity as loving as I thought God to be would show me sign after sign like that and then take this longed-for blessing away from me. Nor would He let it be stolen. I had to try to keep up hope that God would set things right, not just because I felt called to do so, but because the implications of God's refusal (or inability) to help me were too devastating to even consider.

Unfortunately, this time my hope turned out to be misplaced. There wasn't one particular day when I woke up and realized that God wasn't going to come through for me, but after about a month of no word from Him or Chris, even I could no longer keep up my dutiful optimism without feeling like a fool. No amount of prayer, no amount of trying to bargain with the Lord or remind Him of my faithfulness or desperately demonstrate my trust that He would come through with the gift He'd so clearly indicated was mine ever changed anything. The truth was that Chris was gone, and I had to admit there was no reason for me to keep believing he'd be coming back.

Once I surrendered to that reality, the direction of my accusations shifted. It was no longer Chris I blamed, but God.

I'd been set up and torn down; I felt as though my beautiful, admirable faithfulness had been taken advantage of. I'd cried myself into dehydration and worn out my friends' capacity to commiserate with me and failed to negotiate any leniency from my professors as I struggled to focus on life outside of my pain and confusion, and still no mercy had come. I pictured God watching all of it, knowing well and good not only what had happened to me but all that I felt about it. I imagined Him listening to my pleas, hearing me beg for clarity or even just a little comfort, and choosing to not even reach out a hand.

Being rejected by Chris was one thing, but to have my devotion to the Lord go unreciprocated on top of that was beyond what I could handle, logically and emotionally. I was baffled. I felt deeply wounded. I was inexpressibly disappointed. But most of all, I was mad.

I mean, I was fucking angry.

THE WAY I'd been raised had etched into me certain expectations. Not just expectations about what life would look like for me, a young woman eager to jump on the bandwagon of marriage and children and all that, but expectations about what God was capable of doing—and standing by, ready to do—in my life. Expectations that preachers and teachers had carefully instilled over two and a half decades. Expectations that gave me hope that, no matter the situation, divine intercession was possible and could overcome human whims. In expecting that God would follow through with what I believed he'd promised me—namely, tangible love in the form of a romantic partner who would choose me for the rest of his life—I was doing what I'd been told to do: I was daring to believe a miracle could happen.

The Bible stories only exacerbated the issue. There were examples of these kinds of miracles all throughout the Old and New Testaments. I saw them as literal demonstrations of what was possible if you had enough faith. I believed with every fiber of my being that God favored his followers, happily gave blessings to the righteous, and was capable of supernaturally intervening in earthly situations to rescue His children. Why wouldn't the same apply to me?

There was one Bible story in particular that felt especially pertinent to what I was going through after Chris declared he was done with me. I thought of it often and held on to it like a buoy as I tried to keep my head above the rising waters of despair in the weeks after our break-up. It's a tale where, like many of the sacred narratives I was raised with, God takes a while to respond to the pleas of His suffering faithful. Incidentally, it's also a story that the church often uses to address the issue of the anger a believer might feel toward God when circumstances are unjust or things fall apart and God seems far away. I'm talking about the story of Job.

In the story, a character referred to as Satan (a term meaning "the Accuser" or "the Adversary" in Hebrew) bets God that this man, Job, a dedicated worshipper of God, will renounce God if enough shitty things happen to him. God takes Satan up on the wager and allows Satan to kill and steal all of Job's livestock and servants, kill all of Job's children, and make Job ridiculously ill, his body covered with boils and sores.

As a result of all this suffering, Job's wife insists—quite understandably—that he curse God, but Job refuses. Meanwhile, Job's friends assume that he's done something terribly wrong to deserve all this pain, and they insist that he repent.

This he also refuses, standing firm on the fact of his innocence.

He does, however, demand that God explain Himself, and waits stubbornly in his misery until God finally shows up to say, in so many words, "Hey, Job! I created everything around here. What the hell do you know?" In response to God's rebuke, Job apologizes for being so presumptuous, and then he gets back all his stuff as a reward.

The moral of the story, as far as I can tell—and based on how it was taught to me—is that while you may have good reasons to be mad about your life circumstances, sometimes, no matter how tragic your situation, God owes you no answer and will eventually reward you if you find that acceptable.

From where I stand now, there are some things I find very troubling about this narrative. For instance, it seems to teach people that they should take "because I said so" as a satisfactory answer while submitting to a version of love that involves the right to injure at will. At the time of my break-up with Chris, though, I was so focused on figuring out what it was that God wanted from me, on finding a spiritual algorithm that could produce a solution to my agonizing loss, that I was willing to try every tactic I could think of to get some kind of response from my Heavenly Father, including taking a cue from Job.

Like him, I demanded answers. How could something that was so clearly God's will be ruined by the decision of one measly guy? And if God's will could be ruined, and my dreams —the dreams of a faithful woman—destroyed because of one cowardly dude's refusal to follow what was so clearly ordained, then what was the point of having faith at all? What had I been waiting for all those years, if not an acknowledgement of my obedience, a treasure uncovered just in time to show the world that all my seemingly foolish focus on this religion was actually right?

I screamed these questions at God. I bawled them, hyperventilating in my bed or even sometimes on the rough carpet floor of my room when I needed my physical position to match the lowliness of my spirit. Wherever I found myself when the anguish took over, I cried out to God. I didn't care if He came down to scold me for asking the questions so long as, like Job, I got back what I'd lost.

And do you know what God said when He showed up, when He came to me in my misery, as any parent would rush toward their suffering child? As He did however many millennia ago for Job when he was at the end of his rope? It's a trick question, because in my case, God never arrived. He never uttered a word.

I'D NEVER IMAGINED I could feel even more betrayed than I already did, yet there I was, deserted. Chris's irresponsibility was one thing, but for God to stand by and do nothing while my heart was destroyed—for Him to allow me to believe so wholeheartedly that I was on a blessed path, knowing all the while what was going to happen—was something I couldn't comprehend. Even more than being unable to comprehend it, I couldn't accept it. It wasn't just that the situation didn't make sense, which is how I'd felt about all those Christian tenets that confused me and prompted doubt when I was a child; it was that the situation was offensive.

The man I'd literally considered my God-ordained (and well-earned) future husband had just up and walked away, and God had refused to stop it. Of course I was angry—angry not only with the man but with the God who was supposed to keep him there. And if God wasn't going to keep him there—if He was choosing to honor Chris's free will or something like that—then I assumed that at the very least I'd be consoled. That was part of the payoff when it came to all my religious fervor and my various sacrifices, right? To have the Lord of the universe at my side, comforting me in times of devastation? I didn't even have that! So yes, I was mad. And I stayed mad. I'm still a little mad, to be honest.

I realize that saying all this might make it seem like I believed that God was mine to control, that I could force Him to give me what I wanted through my good behavior. That really wasn't the case, at least not in my conscious mind. I would have balked in genuine indignation had you suggested such a thing to me back then. What I did assume, though—again, because I'd been taught it—was that being a Christian meant God and I had an understanding. That with my love and devotion came certain benefits: His protection and His support. This was no different in my mind than what a parent was expected to provide for their child. Yet in that post-breakup moment, when I was in distress, when I needed comfort from the one all-loving and all-powerful being in the universe with whom I thought I had a close personal relationship, there was nothing but radio silence.

You might also be saying to yourself, Grete, this sounds a whole lot like Prosperity Gospel thinking. About that, you would be right. You see, integral to the theology that I was raised in was indeed the understanding that God's rewards for his followers were not just going to come after death in the form of a heavenly paradise, but would also be found in the form of desirable material assets during one's life on Earth. In other words, I was taught that if you were a good Christian, God would make you comfortable.

For many, the Prosperity Gospel has to do with money.

For me, what I wanted (and, again, expected), among other things, was romantic capital. In my patriarchally-molded mind, that was the ultimate in both economic and existential stability. But whether they took the form of money or love, my understanding was that my devotion would earn me gifts from God in this life, here and now. This thinking also led to the conclusion that if I was well-behaved and still not feeling taken care of, something was wrong. For believers like me, life was supposed to be fair.

I don't think the church meant to teach me to be so focused on immediate gratification. I can't count the number of sermons I listened to over the course of my life warning against seeing God as a Santa Claus-type figure (a.k.a. "Vending Machine God", a.k.a. "Fairy Godmother God"). Yet the evangelical communities of which I was a part could not help but imply that we were all following Jesus with the assumption that our lives would be made easier as a result. We were chastised for only loving God because of the blessings He could bestow, yet, at the same time, His blessings were always offered as the primary—if not the only—reason to follow Him. It was a Christianity born of privilege, no doubt.

Problematic as it may have been, that was my theological orientation. And, as a result, when everything with Chris went down the way it did, life suddenly failed to compute. I no longer felt like I had an understanding of who God was, or what He wanted from me. I'd been wrong about what His signals looked like, and wrong about His willingness to vindicate me. Naturally, I had to wonder what else I might be wrong about.

SOME SAY TIME HEALS. Perhaps, rather, time passes, disinterested in our wellbeing, and we simply grow used to the things we find we cannot change. As my eagerness to pass whatever tests I thought God might be administering faded, what had felt like a permanent inability to settle back into any semblance of contentment neutralized to a defeated acceptance of the fact that the days were still passing and would probably keep doing so whether I liked it or not. There was no stopping the clock on account of my grief. Acknowledging this, I decided to start taking some genuine interest in my classes, which were in desperate need of my attention. I even managed to make some new friends in Pasadena. I was learning, as I swayed back and forth in the doorway between resentment and release, to embrace my unexpectedly single life far away from home.

God and me, though, weren't doing so well. There had been a falling out, and given that my despondent attempts at our reunification had gone completely ignored, it was proving hard to find the energy to care about getting on the same page with the Lord. A certain spell had been broken. I couldn't manage to get back to the level of focused worship I'd sustained before my heart shattered. Either I hadn't done enough to warrant generosity from God, or all those stories about God eventually coming through for His beloved were fairy tales. I knew for sure the former wasn't true, so I was left with the troubling prospect—dim but growing stronger— that there was in fact nothing special in it for me when it came to living for Jesus.

It was one thing to go through the first step of confronting my doubts, wherein my own intuition balked against difficult teachings and contradictory edicts. Finding equilibrium amid all that turned out to be relatively easy. Who was I, this young, frail human, to presume to know better than the millennia-old wisdom of the church? Who was I to presume that God's judgments of what was right and what was wrong would match up with my mortal perspective? Fair enough. I could choose to humbly defer while I tried to figure out how to come to terms with the tenets that didn't make sense to me.

But my expectations of how God would act toward me, an obedient believer, were a different story. I needed at least to be able to count on Him to conduct Himself as the church told me He would, especially given how much effort I was putting into defending His honor. There was going to have to be some alignment between the reasons I'd been given for following Jesus and the experienced consequences of my faithful life.

From the Break-Up on, church ceased to be a place of comfort for me. It ceased to be the home that it had been, and not because I was no longer attending the congregation where I grew up. On the contrary, I'd always found it easy to fit in at new churches when I was away at college or living abroad. The unease I felt at the various churches I tried out in Southern California—and I tried out many—was not because of unfamiliarity but because of indignation. Each sanctuary I entered was a reminder of God's betrayal. While the people around me worshipped with passion, expressing their devotion to their creator, I seethed silently, refusing to pretend I was okay with the way I'd been treated.

You might wonder why I didn't just give up on church altogether at that point, especially with the pain that it caused me to be there. Why I still showed up every Sunday morning, despite my fury. All I can say is that I'd dedicated my whole life to that institution and based every major decision of my life on its teachings. I wasn't yet able to imagine a life without it. But there was no getting around the fact that something in me had shifted. Even though I kept showing up,

I kept showing up mad. I'd reached a point where, much like Job, I refused to submit. I couldn't suppress or sublimate my anger, and I couldn't ignore it. Though I didn't know at that point what the next step would look like, I knew that moving forward in my quest for truth was the only option. Things would never go back to the way they were before.

HAVING dreams shattered isn't fun, but in this case, I have to admit, I'm glad for it. Unpleasant as it was to live in that pain for an extended period of time, I now know that it was necessary to build the sense of empowerment—the conviction that my experience had to matter, too—that was essential for having the courage to eventually make my departure from the fold. It's what I needed to coax me further along on the path to freedom: freedom from the burden of the church's rigid vision for its members' lives, from the intense constraints of Christianity that left my imagination naïve and my resilience atrophied.

I needed more skepticism, and it wasn't going to come from an intellectual place. As I said before, things had to get personal. The anger that welled up in me as a result of the Break-Up and the fact that I was left to my own devices to make it to the other side of my depression despite my fervent prayers helped me see God from a new, more removed angle—an angle I don't think I would ever have arrived at without being forced to by circumstances beyond my control.

I want so badly to say that I wouldn't wish what I went through on anyone, let alone myself, but I do—with apologies—wish it, in some way, for you. Not a breakup specifically, but whatever it will take to get you to be angry, and stay angry, with God. The details of what brings that about will probably be a little different for everyone. Whatever the situation is that gets you there, my hope is that you too arrive at a place where you are compelled to demand answers to the unfair things, and that you don't take silence as a sign that you should just get over it. That you are pushed to a place where you are desperate enough to realize that God does, in fact, owe you something.

Then, if you can, try sitting in that space for a while, just like we practiced when we paid attention to our doubt. Be willing to be at odds with God Himself, even when the voices of sermons past are trying, like Job's know-it-all friends, to shame you into giving in.

Dare to believe that you deserve a response from your so-called savior. Allow yourself to feel worthy of an answer more substantial than "What do you know?" And, begin to consider what you will do with yourself if you never receive the accounting from the Lord that you are looking for—if all the trust and deference you've invested into following His will is not, in the end, reciprocated in some reasonable way.

STEP 3
MAKE FRIENDS WITH SINNERS

I've always felt a strong identification with misfits. I'm not sure if this is due to my innate personality, the contrast between the peacemaker role I took on in my family system and the rebel I really wanted to be, the fact that I grew up in a town that took great pride in being a haven for the strange, or some combination of all three.

In any case, I never considered myself quite "normal." Indeed, I wasn't normal in many ways growing up—most of them weird as opposed to cool; some of them, like the panic attacks I experienced when I was left alone for more than a minute or two, definitely signs that I could have used a bit of extra support as a child. But I was who I was, idiosyncrasies and all, and while I craved love and acceptance as much as the next kid, I also learned to find a certain virtue in living outside the bounds of the standardized life.

At first, in childhood and even through high school, the differences I lived with were mostly social, and they seemed to happen in ways that were beyond my choosing. It was simply a fact, part of who I was organically, that I never belonged to the A-list group at school, and I was generally okay with that. Apart from an unfortunate attention-hungry phase in twelfth grade during which I abandoned the stalwart crew of friends I'd had since middle school for a chance to eat lunch adjacent to the popular crowd, I felt perfectly at home with the small cadre of welcoming, equally quirky comrades that I met up with every morning on the steps outside of the drama teacher's classroom. Together, we made the most of the freedom to be fully ourselves that steering clear of the spotlight allowed.

Despite my ability to enjoy a life on the fringes of the ecosystem that is high school, I was still pretty conventional in terms of interests and appearance. I dressed how movies and magazines told me to, listened mostly to the music that was on the radio, and was about as well behaved as you could get. It wasn't until I was in college that I really began to embrace the eccentric, not just in terms of who I was hanging out with, but in terms of how I expressed myself.

It might sound like a typical evolution: sheltered kid goes off to undergrad with other young folks from around the globe and her sense of what's possible expands as she encounters diverse perspectives and learns about how small her world actually was when she was back home. For me, though, the experience that blew my mind was a bit of the opposite. It was the mind-numbing uniformity of the institution I chose to attend that compelled me to explore new aesthetic territory. I was working against what I realized I *didn't* want to be as much as I was working toward what I did.

What I had wanted—before I knew what I was in for—was to go to a Christian school that was small, academically rigorous, and by the beach. Having been raised in my own little counterculture-y beach town bubble, completely unaware of what folks in any other part of the country (or even the southern half of my own state) were up to or interested in, I thought that a spot like that would naturally be full of people like me and those I grew up with and around. People who preferred to get their clothes from thrift shops rather than chain stores. People who drove barely running, hand-me-down cars and happily shared whatever change they had on hand with folks living on the street.

Little did I know that the parameters I'd laid out for my dream school would end up taking me to an institution that was also the preferred destination for a whole lot of primarily rich, primarily blonde, primarily conservative, primarily Abercrombie & Fitch-wearing young adults from either the Midwest or Orange County who had everything in common with each other and almost nothing in common with me. My first day on campus was a study in reverse culture-shock. Slowly, it dawned on me that I was a stranger in my own nation. To feel like I had any kind of identity on campus, I knew that I was either going to have to assimilate (a decidedly impossible task) or make myself visible by contrast.

Thankfully, by the wisdom of the housing office or just sheer dumb luck, I ended up spending my freshman year living with some beautifully uncommon young ladies who were a little more self-possessed than I was, quite a bit less fearful of authority, and just as interested in fitting in with the catalog-model masses of our elite college—which is to say, not at all. They wore clothes that they made themselves and listened to Morrissey and one of them even shaved her head one day—a truly courageous feat for a woman in a community like that at the end of the twentieth century. From them, I learned what fun it could be not just to ignore the normal but to challenge it, to get right up in its face with exactly what it was afraid of.

I took the inspiration they handed me and ran with it. In

my sophomore year, I became mildly obsessed with the Sex Pistols. Always in the mood to play with my look thanks to those young women who emboldened me, I started wearing safety pins as earrings in what I thought was a fairly modest homage to punk rock. My ears were already pierced, and I'd sterilized the pins with a lighter before sliding them through the holes in my lobes, so it wasn't quite the brutal gesture it might have appeared. Nevertheless, at my little evangelical liberal arts school with the Ivy League price tag, the makeshift jewelry stood out starkly against a sea of pastel polos and golden promise rings when I walked into the dining commons.

One afternoon, I brought my lunch tray to a group that included a petite, blonde gentleman a year or two older than I who was a particularly proper dresser. Clad in the school's unofficial uniform of a collared shirt and khakis, he noted my safety pin earrings with words that feigned curiosity, but he used a tone that betrayed his judgment and fear. After a brief interaction, he quietly scooted away from me and stayed at the other end of the table for the rest of the meal. I laughed about it afterward and couldn't wait to tell my friends. It was exactly the reaction I'd been hoping to get from the clean-cut masses; I welcomed his revulsion with pride.

Of course, it was easy to feel noble in my edginess in that environment, surrounded by the most traditional of people, and not actually rebelling against anything of substance. Despite my adventures in the moderately provocative, such as when I dyed my hair fire-engine red for a full year or pierced my eyebrow and lip, my version of heresy went only so far. I was still not ready to be an actual rule-breaker, nor was I ready to hang out with the actual rule-breakers. I didn't smoke cigarettes under the bridge at the edge of campus or drive to the local state school to drink and hook up with strangers like the real heathens. In truth, I was scared of them, and even more scared of getting caught. I might have had some nerve when it came to my sartorial choices, but just below the surface I was a people pleaser, terrified of disappointing those who had any semblance of authority over me. I had found a way to be empowered in and by my difference, but I still very much cared about being good.

That all changed after I got angry with God. Fast forward a few years from college to graduate school, where I found myself bobbing in a sea of disbelief, existentially untethered in the wake of that rapid but nasty break-up with Chris. After all of that happened—after I lost my sense of what (and whom) I was actually living for—I was finally ready to try being a person who did what she wanted no matter what others thought. Not yet around my parents, of course, or, heaven forbid, any supervisor at work, but definitely around my peers and definitely, definitely in front of the Lord. What did I owe that inept, sadistic deity anyway, after what He'd let happen to me? It was time, I decided, to have a bit of the worldly fun I'd only been alluding to with my unorthodox fashion choices. It was time for me to see what it felt like to act like I was free.

About a year and a half into my time in Pasadena, just a few months shy of the end of my master's program, I was offered a chance to move out of the apartment I'd been living in since starting seminary. A handful of acquaintances—some of my classmates, plus some friends of theirs—wanted to rent a house together. They'd found an affordable early-1900s Craftsman-style home with seven small bedrooms, driveway parking, and a giant backyard, and they were on the hunt for a couple more people to fill the space. As for me, I was dying to get out of that apartment since all it reminded me of was the heartbreak I'd been through, so I told them I was seriously interested.

The only problem was that going through with this move meant leaving my then-roommate in the lurch. While we weren't best friends (we'd connected through a message board for students looking for school housing before the start of our first term), we were friendly, and she was incredibly loyal. She'd put up with a lot, trying to support me through my post-breakup confusion. Considering how many hours I spent in that apartment not wanting to live, I can only imagine how many hours she spent not wanting to live with me. But she stuck it out and, as far as I know, assumed we'd be living together until we were done with our two-year programs.

Unfortunately, I was not committed to the same premise. I'd assumed that we would stay in the same place if nothing else came along, and barring an unforeseen emergency, there was no way that I was going to take off in the middle of the original one-year lease. But when the chance to move into the big house presented itself, we were at the point where our legal obligation was only month-to-month, which meant that both she and I were within our rights to leave as long as we gave thirty days' notice. Nevertheless, I sensed that a decision to move out before graduation was not going to go over well with her, even if it was contractually valid.

I had a serious choice to make. On the one hand, I could prioritize the peace and stability of my roommate by passing up the opportunity to move. Doing so would avoid a mess and keep me in her good graces. It was also what I'd been trained to do as a good Christian woman: to sacrifice my pleasure for the sake of others' tranquility. On the other hand, I had a strong feeling that the opportunity to move was not something I could let pass by out of fear of conflict. Something in me knew that this house might change my life, if only I could be brave enough to walk away from what was comfortable and risk being seen as improper.

Before I made my final decision, I conferred with my mom, just to make sure I wasn't doing a completely shameful thing. She agreed that while more time to search for my replacement in the apartment would have been ideal, sometimes life just doesn't work out like that, and I was within my rights to leave because I was giving the required amount of notice. She also said that it sounded like moving into the new house was something I was really excited about, and that I shouldn't let a perceived obligation get in the way of what I wanted for myself.

Feeling fortified by my mother's words, I let the folks who were going to rent the house know that I was officially in and then found the moment—and the courage—to tell my roommate I was leaving. The announcement was not well received, to say the least. At first she was surprised, which I expected; then, the anger set in. I had prepared myself as best I could to receive her displeasure, but it was still painful to stand there and listen to her side of the story and remain committed to my decision.

While I didn't believe that I was duty-bound to live in that apartment until we both made plans to leave at the same time, I did have sympathy for the inconvenience I was causing. For one thing, the apartment we were living in was school-run housing, which meant that it had to be a fellow student who moved in. Plus, I was going to be moving out at the end of February, which is not exactly a peak time for housing transitions in the academic year. It was going to be difficult to find a person to take my spot, and not just any person—a person my roommate wanted to live with. The other option was for my roommate to move out simultaneously, but this was no less disruptive a situation given that the prospect was being sprung on her out of nowhere.

After the initial shock and indignation at my news wore off, she asked me to reconsider. I agreed, thinking it probably wasn't a good idea at that moment to say that I'd already spent quite a bit of time weighing the consequences of my choice and there wasn't really anything left to think about on my end. Out of respect for her request, I took another day to ponder my choice. As I expected, by the end of those twenty-four hours, I came back to what I'd already decided: I had to do what I had to do.

Well, that's not quite accurate. I wanted to do what I wanted to do, and I was going to do it, because that big, beautiful house with those fun, alluring people seemed like a stroke of luck I not only had very much earned, but also might never encounter again. So, I chose to do the selfish thing. I chose to be disappointing. And that decision—the decision to do what felt right instead of what looked good—turned out to be one of the best and most significant of my life.

We called it the Green House, on account of the chalky forest shade the exterior stucco had been painted. I don't remember who helped me move in, though somebody must have; there's no way I got my queen size bed and hardwood dresser from my old apartment to my new upstairs bedroom all by myself. I just remember *being* there. It was almost like I'd always lived there, ever since I came to Pasadena, and everything that happened before—the weekends spent driving to Orange County, the Break-Up, that awkward final month trying to live peacefully with my now ex-roommate—was just a bad dream.

It was in this house, with its strange, closet-less rooms and its front porch on which I'd spend many a wine-fueled evening with friends, that I was exposed to a joy for life that was deeper and more sincere than anything I'd experienced in the communities that called themselves Christian. In this house, I learned what it meant to love people for who they were rather than who you thought they needed to be, and I learned what it looked like when a person was actually set free by that kind of love. Most remarkably of all, the people I learned these things from were the very people I'd spent so long being intrigued by but too scared to approach and unsure how to act around. They were the religious misfits. They were what the church called sinners—or rather, they were living in sin.

Now, any Christian worth their salt will tell you that we're all sinners. That's kind of the whole reason for the religion in the first place. So, it's not like I genuinely believed I wasn't a sinner and other people were. But it's also true that, when it comes to how they think about the people around them, many Christians—especially those of the evangelical variety—do categorize certain folks as "living in sin." Being a sinner is, according to most branches of Christianity, inherent to being human: We have all screwed up by violating God's will for our lives, and we will all screw up again, regardless of our best intentions. Hence the need for God's forgiveness, via Jesus' sacrifice, when the screw-ups happen. People living in sin, however, are actively and persistently choosing to go against God's will and don't seem interested in changing their ways or expressing any kind of remorse.

Pretty much all non-Christians fall into the "living in sin" category, but it can also contain believers who are not making decisions about their daily behavior in accordance with the church's ideas about right and wrong. Things like premarital sex, smoking, excessive drinking, excessive cursing, definitely drug use, and definitely any kind of non-heteronormative or non-cisnormative behavior were all considered anathema by the Christians I grew up with.

You might notice that something like hoarding wealth is not on that list, which is interesting considering how much Jesus spoke about material resources and what to do with them. In truth, holding onto more than you need while others around you go without was not a habit that was openly criticized in the church that helped raise me—a church that, incidentally, counted among its members the owners of some of the most successful businesses in our small city. What I *had* been taught was that, whether you were a self-proclaimed believer or not, choosing to engage in those more traditional vices was choosing a life of separation from the Lord.

Then I moved into the Green House, and for the first time in my life I found myself part of a community where the people I spent all my time with were participating in some combination of those supposedly sinful activities on a regular basis. Some of these folks were believers, some were atheists, and some were somewhere in between, but all were, in their own ways, disinclined toward what the evangelical church considered righteous living. I, on the other hand, had not been in the habit of making those kinds of choices. I was "good," because I was afraid. Aside from routine masturbation—which, thanks to purity culture, I genuinely thought was perverted and hated myself for just about every day of my life—the most judgment-worthy thing I'd done up to the point when I moved into the house was to opt out of a living arrangement with barely enough notice.

Generally speaking, I had never lived in sin. And because I

was a coward, I hadn't been very interested in doing so either—until I got pushed out of my cozy little nest of self-righteousness by the realization that God might not be everything I'd always been told He was. I was scared of getting in trouble. I was scared of something terrible happening to me as a result. I was also under the impression, thanks to my religious indoctrination, that people living in sin were secretly miserable.

LIKE JUST ABOUT every person raised in Christian evangelicalism, I was taught growing up that no matter how much fun someone might look like they're having on the outside, it's impossible for a person to be both living in sin and truly happy. It's the same tactic used by your average after-school special, right? Sure, those kids smoking in the parking lot act like they're having a good time, but just wait until you see what their lungs look like in this x-ray! Only, in the case of the sinner, the decay we were most concerned about was spiritual. I'd been persuaded that it was literally impossible for someone to engage in any behavior that God (according to the church's teachings) disapproved of and not be tormented on the inside.

The problem was, this information was secondhand. The folks the church was presuming to know—the people who got high or hooked up or were openly gay—were not asked about how they were feeling, whether they were happy or not. The only time anyone was brought in to share about their personal experience with "sin" was in the context of a testimony, where the whole point was for the speaker to tell the story of how they were on a path they didn't like (a path of partying and sexual deviance, usually) and eventually found peace in Jesus. But no one ever stood up in front of the congregation and said, "Hey, sometimes I drink 'til I'm drunk and I don't feel guilty about it; or I have sex with people I'm not married to, and I enjoy it."

Of course, even if they had, we Christians would have refused to accept their perspective as legitimate, since in our minds they were just flagrant sinners. Ours was a closed system, meant to control behavior through fear and shame. Even worse, it allowed us participants to feel like we were equipped to judge the interior well-being of folks we did not know based solely on the behavior we saw them engaging in on the outside.

But I was fortunate. Those rule-bucking folks the church was presuming to know? The folks who were attractive to me because of their outsider status but who also felt separate from me because my mind was so narrowed by doctrine? They became my chosen family when I moved into the Green House. Some of them lived there, some of them might as well have, and some just came around now and then. Whatever the frequency of my interactions with any one person, as I became friends with these so-called sinners, the cumulative effect of our time together was powerful enough to begin to counter the hubristic teachings I'd received throughout my youth.

I saw that I'd been wrong to deem them unhappy, that I hadn't known what I was talking about when I told myself that their life choices were soul-destroying. Whether I found myself on the front porch on a chilly night with a small gathering of folks who were chatting about school and work and God while the smoke from our shared hookah swirled around our heads, or found myself alone, knocking on my housemate's bedroom door, hoping she was home, knowing I could trust her to hold space for my pain as I vented about the terrible date I'd just been on, I never experienced anything but welcome and support from my little hedonistic community. Even in the less than enjoyable moments, like when we were all hungover and had to clean up after one of our infamous Halloween parties that had gone until 3 a.m. the night before, there was never any sense that we were missing out on something better, and never any judgment of ourselves or one another. It was okay to have a good time—more than okay, it was important.

That's not to say there were no boundaries, that we were cool with everyone doing whatever they wanted. But rather than those perimeters being drawn by faceless agents of hierarchy who used ancient texts to justify homogenizing regulations that kept the already-powerful in control, our limits for individual behavior grew out of a desire for each person's well-being and the health of the community as a whole. We tried to pay attention to each other's—and our own—comfort levels, and tried to protect one another when lines were crossed. What we had wasn't utopia, but it wasn't bedlam, either.

It was also profoundly enlightening for me. What I experienced living in that house belied the narrative I'd been reciting to myself since I was young: that I would always be safer and happier doing what the church told me to. And since what I'd been telling myself for all those years was simply a repetition of ideas that had been handed to me by the church itself, the truth of the situation—the joy and sense of empowerment that I saw in the eyes and heard in the voices of these friends I had the great luck to end up living with and around—only served to make the possibility that I'd been duped by Christianity all the more apparent.

I was coming to understand the real reason why the church didn't want me hanging out with these people: not because they would drag me down, but because they would help set me free. The church wasn't worried about my happiness (especially not as a woman); it was worried about losing my buy-in. Getting up close and personal with people who were said to be living in sin was verboten because it would give me a chance to compare my experiences to theirs, and in doing so the Christianity I was raised with would be revealed for the domineering, unnecessarily difficult thing that it is.

I'VE FOCUSED a lot on the idea of sin so far, but the key concept here—the key, in fact, to this whole step—is really friendship. Nothing would have ever shifted in my beliefs about the world if I hadn't sincerely opened my heart to this crew of iconoclasts and taken them at their word about their own lives rather than assuming, like my younger self would have, that they were misguided from the jump. It was crucial that I moved into that house ready to learn rather than eager to teach.

Unfortunately, it's pretty standard for evangelicals to look at their web of social connections as a missionary field. I mean, if you genuinely believe that people will suffer for eternity if they are not right with God when they die and that it's your responsibility to make sure that doesn't happen, then of course you would do everything within your power to convince the folks you care about that they need Jesus. And even if you're an evangelical who isn't driven by actual panic over the souls of the unsaved, you're probably still inclined to see nonbelievers as projects, which brings the element of entertainment into the mix. After all, Jesus did tell his disciples to go out and fish for people, which—in my experience anyway—makes it really easy for the church to turn evangelism into a sport.

Seen only through such a lens, the full, complex personhood of the other is lost, and their status vis-à-vis God is all that remains. The multifaceted individual is reduced to a simple target: salvation. And in that kind of situation, even if the believer's intentions are good, I'm not sure that true friendship is possible.

That's not to say that I never cared for the folks in my life who I thought were living in sin. Throughout middle and high school, most of the people I hung out with outside of church did not share my belief system, and I still loved them dearly. As I've admitted, I had my missionary moments, I tried my hand at conversion. But, looking back, our personal faiths came up pretty rarely in the grand scheme of things. We had, I think, a lot of fun together, and developed deep, sincere bonds over the years despite our differences. All the same, I do wonder what aspects of these friendships were lost—or never present—because I was operating from my evangelical mindset. I wonder if something was missing, if there were things I was unable to give, because of my fundamental belief that these lovely people were living their lives incorrectly. I wonder if they felt a bit judged all the time.

I wouldn't blame them if the answer was yes. I don't necessarily blame my younger self either, because I wasn't yet in a position to question everything I'd been taught about the cosmos. But I do know, thanks to my experiences in evangelicalism, that when I say, "make friends with sinners," the "friend" part might mean something very particular to a certain kind of Christian—something much less vibrant and free than what the average person would imagine a friend to be. So I bring up this point about friendship to specify what needs to happen in this step, especially for those who are actually considering or are already in the process of leaving the church.

You have to check yourself to make sure you're not working from a missionary mindset. You have to be willing to open your mind to the possibility that another person's experience is as real as yours, no matter how different it is than yours. And, you have to be able to—or at least try to, no matter how much it challenges the theology with which you were raised—believe a person when they say they're happy living outside the rules that the church insists God wants us to obey.

You also have to be wary of using people as tokens. It's easy for people in positions of privilege to say, "I have a friend who belongs to this particular marginalized group, and so that is proof that I am accepting and loving of that marginalized group." In that scenario, the person from the dominant group feels both proud and assuaged by the relationship: proud that they come off as inclusive and fair-minded by associating with the individual, and assuaged because now they no longer have to consider themselves complicit in the forces that are marginalizing the other person in the first place. I've been guilty of this in my own life; I imagine I still am sometimes. It took working through a lot of naïveté and ignorance about my own privilege to get to the point where I was capable of being true friends with folks whose perspectives and experiences are very different than my own, and I could identify when I was using their presence in my life as some sort of subconscious ego boost.

As with missionary friendships, the tokenizing friendship (if we can call it a friendship) won't be sufficient to get you to the third step. In that kind of relationship, there is a wall that is still up—there is a lack of self-examination, and an unwillingness to be changed by the other person. But making friends with sinners means that the sinners are your actual friends, not just some folks with whom you have a social connection that makes you feel more down-to-earth than your most uptight Christian counterparts but who are not actually integrated into your private life. When I say make friends with sinners, I'm talking about building a camaraderie with people because you've chosen to significantly change, or to be open to changing, the way you relate to and experience the world. Out of those friendships, if they are organic and true, will come a revelation. And, as a result of that revelation, you might find that some significant assumptions you had about the way the world works have dissipated and left you yearning to learn more about what a life outside of the church would really involve.

LOOKING BACK on this specific moment in my life, I try to measure what it meant for me, a Christian steeped in evangelicalism, to hear about the profound relief that one of my housemates, who had also been raised in evangelicalism, finally found in atheism. What it meant for me to see my gay friends rejecting the premise that their natural attractions were wrong and that they were supposed to be suppressing their own humanity, and instead living in freedom as a result of their self-affirming stance. What it meant for me to be around unmarried women my age who had sex without shame, and talked openly about it. What it meant to live with and around folks who prioritized honesty, generosity, independence, and pleasure over propriety, obedience, fear, and judgment.

In truth, it meant everything. It meant, first, that so much of what I'd been taught was wrong. I was beginning to suspect it, of course, and thanks to what happened with Chris I was primed to accept it. But I really did need to see for myself what existence was like for folks on the other side of the church-centered life, if not on the other side of belief. What I found was that, at the very least, it wasn't the hell-on-earth about which I'd been warned. Quite the opposite, in fact. Sure, people are people, no matter their religious convictions, and everyone has good days and bad days and joys and dark times. But as I became friends—true friends—with folks refusing to be bound by arbitrary, patriarchal rules about what to do with their bodies and where to spend their time, I realized that life is in fact more enjoyable when you get to decide for yourself how you want to live it. Even more than enjoyment, there is peace—the peace that comes from not feeling the need to judge yourself or others in the present moment out of fear that a terrifying, angry God is going to do it later anyway.

Being a part of that community, being fortunate enough to partake in those friendships and witness what I did, also meant that I had a new vision for the future. I had in front of me some real-life examples of what my life might look like if I started basing my choices on my own sense of morality instead of the particular version that had been forced on me by the church.

One especially significant aspect of this glimpse into a possible post-Christian life was the fact that I wouldn't have to be alone. Something that kept me and countless other folks tied to religion, even when we were past the point of personal belief, was the fear of the loss of community. By its very nature, church facilitates relationships; it provides people to go through life with. Before the friends I made through the Green House, I'd been unable to envision a social network outside of Christianity that could feel as present and committed as what I'd found in church. But thanks to my openness to a new kind of company, and my new friends' willingness to embrace me, insecurities and all, I knew that I'd have plenty of folks waiting for me on the other side of faith.

Another thing I could see was what it looked like to be truly free to love—love yourself, and love others. That was something I wanted so badly, and it was something I had struggled to find in the church.

I had always been instructed to live my Christian life in such a way that nonbelievers would be envious of what I had (namely, Jesus) and ask how they could get it too. But after years spent trying to reconcile my doubts and my more recent efforts to push through the deep resentment I had toward God after the blueprint I'd drawn up for my life was shredded, *I* was the one looking at my friends who were rejecting church traditions and feeling like *I* wanted what *they* had.

I was tired of being anxious about being bad. I was tired of trying to justify to myself the acceptance of rules I simply could not understand, such as when congregations claimed to love LGBTQ+ folks but put limits on the extent to which they were allowed to be involved in the community. I was tired of policing my own and others' behavior for the sake of some reward—or for the fear of some punishment—that I now suspected might never come.

I was ready to let go.

However, given how deeply my identity was entwined with the church and how early on in the process of leaving I still was at this point, for better or worse, letting go did not yet mean walking away altogether. I was prepared and eager to release my strict evangelical ideas about purity and sin, but I still wanted to see if there was a way to do so and keep the best of what the church had to offer me—if there was a way to stay a Christian but be cool.

To that end, I decided to make a drastic change in the type of church I attended, taking a hard left turn from evangelicalism into Anglicanism. I'd heard about an Episcopal congregation just a few blocks away from where I lived that was infamously liberal, and I decided to accompany one of my housemates, who was himself trying it out, one sunny Sunday morning.

From the moment I walked through the heavy wooden doors that led to the nave, I knew that I'd found my new spiritual home. Something about the formality of the service and being surrounded by beautiful stained glass on every side made me feel like I could hold my own emotional space during services. It felt more solemn and removed, less invasive of my spirit, in contrast to the complete surrender encouraged by the blank walls and aw-shucks attitude of the evangelical churches that I knew so well. I was also relieved to find that this church was enthusiastically affirming of LGBTQ+ people, gender inclusive at all levels, proud to proclaim their allegiance to immigrants and refugees, and disinterested in supervising what an individual chooses to do with their body.

However, the congregation was also, as far as I could tell, largely white and largely wealthy, so it's not like they'd achieved some transcendent, superhuman status as a group. But their ideology was a welcome departure from what going to church had looked like for me in the past. I felt safe there—safe to ask questions, safe to be mad at God, safe to live a life my old churches would have classified as sinful.

For quite a while, I thought that I'd found the answer to my question about whether I could both follow my heart and be a Christian. If I could stay in this church—or one just like it

—forever, the answer would be yes. Considering that the end of this book is given away in its title, we all already know that that's not what happened. Nevertheless, it was an incredibly special space for which I will always be grateful, even if it ultimately turned out to be transitional.

ONCE AGAIN, I find myself near a loss for words. It's difficult—though I'm certainly giving it my best shot—to express just how much better life gets when you try your turn at not being so much of a rule-follower. When you take a chance on not living like there's someone waiting to punish you at the end of every day, let alone the end of your life.

The habit's never truly gone, of course; there is still a part of me that's terrified of getting in trouble with someone, even if that someone isn't God. But you can make conscious decisions here and there to combat that tendency. You can learn to be attuned to the ways you hold yourself back for fear of being—or being seen as—bad, and you can take small chances with your pristine reputation for piety to figure out if life on the sensual side is really as terrible as you've been taught.

It can be scary, for sure. It's like swimming out into water that you can't see the bottom of. Luckily, there are people already out there, splashing around, having a good time. They can encourage you, they can support you, they can offer you company in unfamiliar territory and even teach you some tricks along the way. But you do have to trust them. If they say the water feels nice, you have to risk believing them, even if you've been warned about how miserably cold it is at least once a week for your whole entire life. And if they say there aren't any monsters under the surface, you have to risk believing them, even if the folks you've been hanging out with on the shore have been telling you all about the monsters in gory, scary detail since the day you were born.

If you want to experience actual freedom from judgment, if you want to experience freedom from useless fear, if you want to find out whether what you've been taught about morality and the absolute necessity of Christianity holds up outside the church bubble, go risk making friends with the people who have dared to jump off the dock. Life out there in the open water is not perfect, but at least no one's pretending that it's supposed to be. And soon, if you really are willing to change your mind about what it is we're all supposed to be doing with the brief time we have on this beautiful planet, the word "sinner" will transform in your mind from a sad, scornful judgment—a symbol of everything you think you need to avoid—to a term of endearment, a badge worn with pride because it means you've renounced the powers that keep us separated from each other and from our own selves.

ONE MORE THING before we move on: Because of the joy and comfort found here in step three, where you've opened your heart to the folks you'd previously been scared of and hopefully stopped being so critical of your own behavior too, it's tempting to stay in this spot for a while. In fact, some folks never leave. They find a balance between a Christian life and a self-directed one, typically integrating into a liberal-leaning congregation like the Episcopal one I attended for some time.

If that's the place for you, fantastic. I know a lot of people who love it there. My goal in writing about this process is not to convince you to abandon your faith even if you want to hold on to it. That would make me no different than the folks who convinced me that it was my job to keep my heart walled off from everyone who lived and thought differently than I did.

All the same, there might come a day—or perhaps it's already come—when you begin to wonder what the relevance of religion is to your life, especially when the rules you thought applied no longer do. When you begin to ask yourself where the misinformation stops: If the church was wrong about the destructive nature of so much of what they claim is sinful, you might think, what else are they lying to me about, intentionally or not?

If you do reach that point, if you are asking yourself that question, then you might be ready to take things a little bit further. Should that be the case, then—as my childhood camp counselors would say—it's time to go back to your bunks and get your Bibles, because the next leg of the journey involves digging deep into the very foundations of the faith we chose, or were skillfully convinced, to build our lives upon.

STEP 4
STUDY THE BIBLE

I've mentioned that I was in seminary for a couple of years in my mid-20s, but I haven't yet gone into detail about how it affected me. Clearly there were events happening at that time in my life—namely, the Break-Up and my eventual move into the Green House—that furthered me on my journey away from the church. But at the same time that those things were chipping away at my relationship with God, I was spending the bulk of my days engaged in an in-depth study of Christian theology. Indeed, the onset of my profound skepticism about the faith in which I was raised coincided with me offering up two whole years of my life to fall even more deeply in love with it. At least, that is what I assumed my professors hoped would happen for me and my fellow students.

To my surprise, the seminary I attended did not seem as interested in indoctrination as the churches and evangelical organizations in which I'd previously participated had been. Yes, the faculty and staff were passionate about their faith—after all, they'd dedicated their professional lives to the study of its intricacies. But I quickly found that the school was a space for questioning as much as it was a space for devotion. Furthermore, even though it was an exclusively Christian institution, it acknowledged a variety of approaches to that particular belief.

I also discovered, once I arrived on campus and started chatting with other students who were more familiar with the world of theological studies than I, that the school had something of a reputation in conservative church circles, and not necessarily a good one. The institution was by no means liberal relative to the secular world, but it turns out that, by the strange logic of evangelicalism, it was considered fairly progressive compared to other Christian seminaries I might have attended. As you can imagine, in this context "progressive" is not a compliment.

I spoke with a number of classmates whose family members and friends from back home had warned them that attending our particular school would lead them away from God. In fact, I had a friend of my own from back home—someone who tended to be much more conservative in his interpretation of the Bible than I was—who said that his Biblical studies professors from college had cautioned him about the dangerous textual analysis that was happening at the seminary I was going to.

I laughed him off in the moment, just as I tilted my head in confusion when my fellow students told me that the pastors from their home churches were worried about them turning liberal if they came to this school, but it turns out that those professors and pastors were right to be suspicious. The historical-critical approach that our seminary took to Biblical studies, where the text is examined in light of its time period, geography, and culture of origin, revealed a lot about the Bible that only furthered my doubt about the veracity of everything I'd been taught by the church.

Like most evangelicals, I'd been raised to read the Bible as if it was any other book. I thought that, save for the occasional piece of ancient terminology that required a footnote, the meaning of the words on the page was evident: all I had to do was read them. The idea that my living in the United States around the turn of the 21st century and coming from a European heritage would have any impact on my ability to understand what was really going on in this book never occurred to me. If it was inspired by God, even though it was written by humans, it transcended context, didn't it?

Not quite. But before I get into what exactly it was that I learned about the Bible in seminary that contributed to my withdrawal from Christianity, I'm going to take some time to share a bit about what brought me, an English major and aimless creative type, to such an institution in the first place.

IT STARTED WITH A DREAM. Ever since I'd returned from that six-month stint with the international missionary organization in the spring of 2005, I'd been wondering what was next for my life. At the time, I was nearly twenty-four years old, nearly two years out of college, and committed to self-improvement but wanting a long-term vision for the future.

Graduate school was a natural choice for the next stop in my journey. I'd always thrived in academia, and I wanted to become more specialized. In what, though, I didn't yet know. I just knew that I'd studied English in college because I loved discussing and writing about literature, and why not study what you love if you're going to pay—or borrow—that much money for it?

The downside was that being an English major didn't leave me with much direction when I graduated. I still didn't know what I wanted to do with my life besides fall in love and get married, and those were givens. I needed something that would set me on my own unique career path, something that would funnel me into the natural next steps toward a fulfilling job, whatever that ended up being.

A number of ideas crossed my mind. There was the option to continue what I'd started—to get a master's or even a PhD in literature. But somehow I already knew, even without experiencing it first hand, that studying that subject at that level was a much more serious game than what I'd enjoyed in undergrad. I had a hunch that the elitism would be rampant, the feedback would be brutal, and that everything I'd loved about my English classes up to that point would be missing or stolen from me by the time I was done. It just didn't seem like my cup of tea. Based on what I can tell from friends and acquaintances who've earned doctorates in literature since then, my reservations were not entirely off-base.

I also considered studying photojournalism. It sounds random, I know, but I'd become interested in photography in college and found out that I had a decent talent for it. I figured that I could combine that budding skill with my already well-developed writing abilities and take a chance on what seemed like a truly dreamy career. I mean, traveling all the time, sharing stories in artistic ways, helping raise awareness of interesting people and important situations all over the world —why not give it a shot?

I began doing some research, and though I discovered that there weren't many graduate programs in photojournalism in the United States, I did come across one in particular—in Montana, I believe—that seemed appealing. It was while I was in the process of wading through a bunch of informational material about the Montana program that a different idea found me. A much different idea.

One night, in the fall of 2005, months before I reconnected with Chris, I dreamt that a female acquaintance of mine from college came to me and told me that I needed to go to seminary. I woke up the next morning with not only a clear memory of the dream, which wasn't unusual for me, but also a powerful feeling that it hadn't been just a random product of my imagination. As you've probably gathered by now, I'm a bit of a sucker for a sign, and this situation was no different. I had a nagging sense that something or someone beyond my brain was trying to send me a message.

Seminary had crossed my mind before as an option for grad school. I had a handful of friends from college who were doing it, and having a religious angle to whatever I chose as my professional direction wasn't out of the question for me. Plus, learning more about theology in a scholarly setting sounded intriguing, since most of my education about Christianity had been pretty informal. But I knew I didn't want to be a pastor, and I couldn't imagine what other career it could lead to, so up until the night of the dream, I'd not bothered to investigate the notion any further.

Once the dream happened, though, I couldn't shake the feeling it had given me—a feeling like I was being presented with some sort of destiny. I decided that a little bit of research couldn't hurt and started looking around for not terribly conservative schools that offered programs beyond just preparation for preaching. The one I found that intrigued me most—the one I ultimately ended up attending—prided itself on being unattached to any particular denomination and had a very intriguing master's program that combined the studies of theology and art.

At the time, still coming from an evangelical context,

ecumenism did feel like a fairly liberal stance. And, as a person who had her doubts about the more stringent rules and judgments I'd encountered in the church up to that point, I considered such a thing a point in favor of this school. As was the fact that it was in California—I was comforted by the idea of not having to leave the coast. But it was the pairing of theology and art that attracted me most of all. Maybe, I thought, there was some way to work for a church or a Christian organization that focused on the arts, thus combining two major interests in my life.

The unfortunate thing was that they didn't offer much in the way of financial aid. Being a seminary, it was a private school, so the cost was all but prohibitive, especially since I was dead set on not taking out any more student loans. Nevertheless, I decided to apply, thinking that if that dream really was a sign from God then the money would work itself out, as I'd been told money magically did by many a pastor over the course of my young life.

Truthfully, I wasn't too worried about it. Because the idea had occurred to me out of nowhere and it didn't really feel like I'd thought of it myself—at least not consciously—I wasn't particularly attached to the prospect of getting into or even going to the school. I simply sent my materials in and waited to see what would happen.

In line with that state of ambivalence, when I received notice about six months later that I'd been accepted into the program, I was pleased but not ecstatic. It was still beyond my ability to afford, and I remained unconvinced that a degree in theology was something that I wanted to pursue. Then, two weeks after I received news of my acceptance, someone from the school called me to tell me that I'd also be getting significant financial aid in the form of a full-tuition scholarship.

This was an enormous surprise to me. I hadn't applied for any scholarships; I didn't even know that they were being offered. The school certainly hadn't advertised them. When I communicated my bewilderment to the woman who'd called me with the good news, she told me that the school itself took the initiative to look through the files of incoming students to identify those who met the qualifications for the scholarship. No separate application (or, apparently, even knowledge of the existence of the award) was required.

As far as I was concerned, the money was a confirmation that seminary was indeed God's plan for me, that the dream hadn't been random. Even though studying theology hadn't been a part of what I'd imagined for myself when I was fantasizing about where to steer my life next, I felt that I couldn't deny how smoothly things were coming together, and I couldn't reject such a generous offer as that scholarship—one I wasn't likely to find elsewhere. I accepted, and the next phase of my journey began.

WHEN I STARTED my theology program the following fall, at twenty-five years old, I considered myself no stranger to studying the Bible. I might not have done it in accredited classes led by folks who had terminal degrees in the field, but I'd listened to Bible-based sermons at least twice a week for most of my life, done about a year of close-reading Gospel studies with a group of fellow twenty-somethings from my home church when I was just out of college, and spent hours each day for three straight months diving deep into the scriptures when I was in the missionary school training on the other side of the world. I'd also managed to read through the whole Bible, cover-to-cover, every word, in sequential order like a regular book. It took a while, but I wanted to be able to say that I'd done it.

Given all that, when I arrived at seminary, the Biblical studies classes in particular—along with those in ancient languages and systematic theology—were the ones I was least excited about. They seemed old hat to me by that time. I wanted to get them out of the way so I could get to the good stuff: the more philosophical (and, to my mind) creative topics like what role art has played in Christianity throughout history, or how theology interacts with and informs popular culture.

It turned out that the specific track I chose didn't require that I study Greek or Hebrew, and I was glad about that, but I was required to take at least four Bible-focused courses. I approached them the way that I'd always approached any class in school, regardless of my interest in the topic: with the intent to do my best. At the same time, I didn't walk in the door with enthusiasm or even much curiosity. Those Biblical studies classes weren't why I was there, and I already knew what I was going to be taught.

Or so I thought. My first quarter, I took a class called something like "Introduction to the New Testament." I can't recall many details. Those first couple of months I was totally distracted by my relationship with Chris. But there was one lecture that I still remember vividly because I was so startled by what the professor said. We were going over some verse about death and resurrection—not Jesus' death and resurrection, but what happens to us humans, particularly us believers, after we die. Out of nowhere, and quite casually, the professor said that he didn't believe in an afterlife. He said, "I think, maybe, when you're dead, you're dead," and that, in his estimation, what Christianity conceptualizes as an eternal soul isn't something that literally exists.

If I wasn't listening very carefully before, he certainly caught my attention in that moment. I was stunned and confused. How was it possible for a Christian not to believe in heaven and hell? Weren't these things everywhere in the Bible? Yet he shared his perspective with such calm confidence. He knew that what he was saying was controversial, and he didn't expect everyone to accept it, but the assuredness he seemed to have in this unlikely opinion was intriguing. He wasn't trying to convince us, I don't think—it seemed, instead, like he was offering a glimpse into a different way of thinking, and we were free to take it or leave it as we saw fit.

He had his reasons for believing such things, of course. Noticing that he'd ruffled some feathers when he made his statement about there being no soul, he took a moment to further explain his position. As I listened, I learned that it's actually not so cut and dry, what the Bible says about the afterlife. Sure, reading the text through a lens clouded by centuries of Christian theological development—all of which is dramatically shaped by surrounding cultures, politics, and the fight for the church's continued existence (if not reign)—you assume certain things are in there because you've always been told they are. But then you look more closely, and you find—as I did, with the help of this professor—that, even with a handful of gospel verses being commonly translated to imply that this place called hell is a place of perpetual, unimaginable suffering, most of your ideas about the afterlife are based more on Dante's *Divine Comedy* than they are on the scripture itself.

He spoke about the ancient Jewish concept of *sheol*, the underground dwelling of the dead, where all deceased people go to reside after they pass away and which, in his explanation, does not in and of itself exist as a place of punishment. He said that though the word *"sheol"*—along with its Greek counterpart *"hades"*—has often been translated into the word *"hell"* in English-language scriptures, the Biblical authors would not have meant what we 21st-century Americans imagine as hell when they were writing in their original languages. He also talked about how other belief systems and worldviews, including ancient Greek philosophy, and certain historical events, like the destruction of Jerusalem in 70 CE at the hands of the Romans, came to influence both Jewish and Christian concepts about (and hopes for) the afterlife.

No doubt what I remember learning is a serious simplification of the facts. Despite my degree, I am no Biblical scholar, and I have no expertise when it comes to the Jewish faith. On the contrary, like many evangelicals, though I was led to believe that I was somewhat familiar with Judaism because of what my pastors were taught in seminary by their fellow Christians and then preached to us in turn, the truth is that most of us were—and are—ignorant in this regard. But ignorance is kind of the point here. Despite how incomplete my knowledge of ancient eschatologies is and was, the lesson I learned was that it is not only naïve but downright incorrect, on a factual level, to assume that the ideas we modern readers have about heaven and hell were also ideas held by the writers of the texts that would eventually become the Bible. And, if the Bible is the entire basis for our Christian theology, then we are also naïve and maybe even incorrect to entertain such a vision of the afterlife, period.

SPEAKING of the Biblical authors and their perspectives, did you know that there was a widespread tradition in ancient Mediterranean societies of writing documents under another person's name? In other words, during the times and places where the various parts of the Bible were composed, it was not uncommon for an author to slap a more well-known person's name on their work. It's called writing pseudonymously, and while there are arguments among scholars about exactly which books of the Bible might be pseudonymous, it's widely agreed that at least a handful of them were not written by the men whose names are on them.

My understanding is that the reasons for this method were varied, but the goal wasn't usually to truly deceive or get away with fraud. Today, in the United States, we might condemn the practice as underhanded, but we have to remember, we're talking about a time and a place apart from modern American conceptions of privacy and property. While we can't really know any given author's intention, it seems—according to what my professors shared as I listened intently, gobbling up every word that demystified what I thought was a sacred text—that it was understood that disciples of prominent figures would sometimes write in their teachers' names to help spread the teachers' messages when they were unavailable or had died. In a way, perhaps, this was actually a way of giving them credit, not an attempt at some kind of backwards plagiarism like we might suppose it to be from a contemporary Western view.

Regardless of the authors' motives, the fact that this whole Biblical pseudonymity thing even existed came as something of a shock to me. And I couldn't write it off as wild speculation; this wasn't fringe scholarship. It was all but decided, agreed upon by loads of experts in the matter. So then, what did it mean for my faith? What were the implications, for me, in terms of Christianity?

First and foremost, I was beginning to understand that the Bible was not what it appeared to be—or at least not what I'd been taught to see it as. Sure, the actual identity of the human author of any given text doesn't really matter when you believe it was all divinely inspired anyway. But the revelation that I hadn't been told the simplest of facts about this precious book, when pastors had had decades to share the truth with me, made me wonder what else had been kept from me. It was like when I made friends with people I'd been told were miserable sinners, yet I found out that nothing bad actually happened when I violated the church's vice laws. It made me wonder what other lies I'd been told for the sake of keeping me under control.

It turns out I didn't have to wonder for very long. I soon ended up in an Old Testament survey course where I learned about the issue of genre in the Bible. The professor pointed us to the Book of Daniel and began a lesson about apocalyptic literature. Now, like most folks familiar with the more modern sense of the word, when I hear "apocalyptic" I think about the end of the world. Little did I know that it was, in ancient Judaism and eventually early Christianity, an actual, distinct genre in which authors sought to provide meaning to past events by writing about them from a point of view prior to the event itself. In other words, they wrote about the event and everything leading up to it as if it were yet to happen, as if the author were prophesying about it. In this way, writers could shape a narrative that gave meaning to a history that seemed chaotic and hopeless for everyone going through it at the time. Not only that, but the word that "apocalypse" comes from—the Greek *apokalypsis*—doesn't even have anything to do with the end times. It means something akin to "revelation" or "unveiling."

In relation to the Book of Daniel, I found this information intriguing but not particularly provocative. Like many evangelicals, the New Testament was always my priority. Then the professor started talking about the Book of Revelation, and my mind was once again blown. He told us about a prominent theory that this writing, with its descriptions of supernatural creatures, accounts of natural disasters, and visions of heaven that I always thought were a God-given glimpse into the final days of humanity's time on Earth, was actually a piece from the apocalyptic genre meant to describe the fall of Jerusalem to Rome in 70 CE. That is, according to this theory, the author was writing in symbolic language about a historic event that had already occurred before he wrote about it, not prophesying about the end of the world, which still has yet to happen 2,000 years after he put ink to scroll.

This information was even more difficult to process than the idea of pseudonymous authorship. It was one thing to find out that some of the people who wrote the Bible might have been employing pen names. Again, it was easy to brush that fact off as inconsequential if you believed, as I did, that the Bible was essentially written by the Holy Spirit using human hands. In that case, it didn't really matter whose hands they were. But to be confronted with the idea—once again, the not-even-fringe idea—that the Bible wasn't about what I thought it was about, what I'd been told for nearly thirty years it was about? That opened up a whole new can of worms.

As I made my way through seminary, it became apparent that the Bible wasn't written for me. More and more, I came to see how much this text did *not* transcend the time and place of its creation. On the contrary, this was a collection of stories and letters and poems and prophecies that were clearly products of the cultures from which they emerged. Everything about the Bible was so...contingent. And yet I'd based my entire modern American life on it.

All of these contingencies reminded me of something else about evangelical Christianity that had been bugging me for a long time, something that I mentioned toward the beginning of this book when I was reflecting on my earliest doubts: the idea that everyone on Earth, regardless of when or where they were born or what belief system was common to their culture, needed Jesus in order to be saved. If someone was raised in, say, Buddhism, it did not matter that they might feel as closely tied to that religion as I did to my Christianity. It did not matter, or so I'd been told, whether they truly loved practicing Buddhism, and insisted that they found freedom in it. If they did not accept Jesus as their Lord and Savior, they would end up in hell, because Christianity was the only path to heaven. Those were the rules I was taught.

But where did those rules come from? If the Bible used symbolism in ways I couldn't even understand because the style of writing that was common back then is not used in English language composition today, how was I to trust that I or even the pastor of my church could draw dogma out of it without completely misinterpreting the author's intent? If the writers of the Bible had concepts of the afterlife that weren't anything close to what I'd been taught was fundamentally Christian, and if on top of that there's a good chance that the Book of Revelation isn't even about Judgement Day, then where was the line between human speculation and God-given truth? Why had I never heard about these issues before?

At first, I'd been startled by what was coming out of my Biblical studies classes, but it wasn't too long before my surprise turned to frustration. I was beginning to suspect that I'd been duped. Not entirely, mind you—at this point, my belief in the existence of God was still standing. And perhaps I had not been duped intentionally, though neither ignorance of history nor its intentional omission from sermons and Bible studies was a good look for the church. But regardless of scope or intent, there was no avoiding the reality that my seminary classes were revealing to me how very mundane Christianity was. What a product of humanity it seemed to be—which was, incidentally, the very criticism I'd been taught to level against all other religions.

With all of this information about the real-life context of the Bible being thrown at me, it became hard to hold onto any sense that there was something superior about Christianity compared to other faiths. More and more, the text I'd adored and revered above all others was being stripped of its power in my life. I guess this is what the folks who were wary of the school's historical-critical approach feared: The Bible was being pushed off its pedestal, inch by inch, and with it, my confidence that the church had a monopoly on the truth.

Things were shifting with my faith. I'd been taught that belief in the Christian God was the only solid ground in an unsteady world, but how could that be true when my primary source of knowledge about God was in fact the focus of so much debate between people who were all supposedly believers in the same thing? The cracks in the foundation were beginning to show.

THE FINAL, fatal blow to my view of the Bible as anything other than an artifact of its time came when I learned about canonization. At a certain point, someone had to decide which writings would be included in the collection that Christians came to know as the Bible, as well as what order those writings would appear in. Up until I got to seminary, I hadn't given this process much thought. I guess I had assumed that there wasn't a whole lot to it, and it certainly never occurred to me (because no one in church ever let on that it might be the case) that there were writings that existed that *weren't* chosen. I also had no idea that, to this day, different branches of Christianity maintain different opinions about which writings constitute scripture.

The first thing that struck me when I started to study canonization was that the process took centuries—millennia, if you count the time it took for the Jewish scriptures on which the Christian Old Testament is based to be written and codified. While evidence suggests that by 200 CE there was already some agreement within the early church about which gospels and theological ponderings counted as authoritative, as Christianity became more institutionalized, these things needed to be systematized and set in stone. So, beginning in the fourth century, church leadership held multiple councils and engaged in prolonged debates to determine the line between sacred and heretical in recorded accounts of their God.

Sitting in class and hearing about all of this, I didn't so much care about the details of the timeline itself. The names and dates were quickly discarded from my memory once I'd held onto them long enough to pass my exams. What interested me—and by "interested" I mean kept gnawing at the pleasantly unambiguous image of the Bible I'd had in my mind up to that point—was the fact that there was enough content to argue over that regularly for that long. I thought, if the criteria for inclusion in the canon are so controversial, so not universally evident, even for the folks who are supposedly experts in the subject, then how can I say that the Bible I've been reading or had read to me every day since I could understand words is the Bible I was meant to have? What made the

Catholic canon, which has seven more books in it than the version I grew up with, so wrong? If I'd been raised Catholic, I would've thought the Protestant scripture was lacking. The issue of contingency was raising its ugly head again.

I also wondered about the people meeting long ago in what I imagined to be small rooms with closed and guarded doors, deciding what every believer around the world should and shouldn't consider to be the story of their God. Certainly, they were all people who had some sort of power within the church. Given that, and given that women were being prevented from actively participating in church by the second century despite their integral role not only in Jesus' life but also in spreading the gospel, it seems likely that it was men—only men—who got to determine church canon. This isn't surprising, of course, but considering how much initiative Jesus took to include women in the witnessing and telling of his story, it is pretty ironic.

The other thing about power, aside from the fact that it tends to be exclusive, is that it tends to be addictive. If you have it, and you like it, chances are you're going to avoid doing anything to fundamentally change the system that got and keeps you in that spot. So, assuming the men who participated in the councils that decided what was officially heresy and what was not enjoyed being in positions of power and didn't want the church to change, shouldn't we be worried about a conflict of interest there? That's what I thought, anyway, sitting in that seminary classroom, learning about how the Gospel of Mary, a piece of writing that was deemed heretical by church leaders, describes Jesus prioritizing a woman over all the other male disciples. And about the Gospel of Thomas—another New Testament reject—that, among other things, seems to champion the idea that Jesus was a philosopher, implying that "the kingdom of God" is an internal state achieved through proper understanding as opposed to a literal postmortem location we're allowed into thanks to Jesus' death and resurrection.

Granted, these two writings appear to have already been considered more or less heretical by some early Christians long before the church was institutionalized enough to be holding meetings on the topic. But it's not like those early Christians weren't interested in political survival as well. There were always multiple takes on this mysterious teacher known as Jesus, especially given how controversial even his most digestible lessons were. Likewise, there were always opinions about which accounts of his actions and ideas were right and which were wrong—someone, or some group of someones, was always going to draw a line indicating inside and outside, blessing and blasphemy.

What I hadn't known, as a trusting, enthusiastic evangelical who was always hearing about the Bible being plain as day on subjects ranging from proper womanhood to the damnation of nonbelievers, was that there were options for what counted as scripture, and that others had already made those decisions for me. Sure, you could argue once again that the Holy Spirit guided the church leaders in their choices about the canon, and in that way the Bible remains the inspired word of God even though it was technically put together by human minds and hands. But the more I learned about how many competing theories there were on all kinds of aspects of the Bible, how many very smart and studied people disagreed with interpretations that had been preached to me my whole life, how inherently political even the earliest Christian institutions were, and how integral the cultures of the authors of scripture were to understanding the manuscripts' true meaning, the more the idea that the Holy Spirit magically overrode all of those things seemed like just an excuse. An excuse to avoid questions about the origins of the theology I'd been told was self-evident in the scriptures. An excuse to keep folks from realizing how much of a leap of faith modern Christianity really is.

To be fair to my younger self, I wasn't completely off-base with the confidence I had in my Biblical knowledge before starting seminary. I'd been able to list all the names of the books of the Bible, in order, since elementary school, and I could recount the plots of many stories from the Old and New Testaments. There were a number of verses I knew by heart, and I'd closely analyzed entire books of scripture, going line-by-line with groups of similarly nerdy friends to observe and interpret what was on the page.

It was understandable that I thought I knew enough about the context, too. Every once in a while, a pastor would throw out a quick lesson about shepherding practices in the ancient Middle East or share some tidbit about Judaism that, though filtered through a Western Christian lens, he hoped might help us better understand the mindset of Jesus and the early church. It seemed like I was getting an education.

Unfortunately, these lessons were deceptive. Not because they were wrong in and of themselves, but because they had me believing there was a profundity to my understanding of the Bible that wasn't truly there. It was only when I really started to dig deep—or when I was compelled to, thanks to my seminary classes—that I realized how much I didn't know. And the combined effect of not only having my own ignorance about the Bible exposed but also learning how much human guesswork was involved in the making and interpreting of so-called scripture gave me a big shove forward on my journey away from the church.

I'd been willing to have faith in something unseen. I'd been willing to choose to believe despite the mystery. I'd been willing to go on an adventure with God. What I realized, though, as I actually studied the Bible, is that I'd been going on an adventure with men—just men—the whole time. Men who failed to disclose information that could have completely changed my understanding of the religion I so vehemently espoused. Men whose perspectives were limited and biased. Men who claimed to be reciting the words of the Lord yet had no proof that what they were saying was more divinely inspired than any other belief system that was doing the same thing.

This realization, and the process that brought me to it, was my fourth step. If we're looking at my story of leaving the church linearly, it's true that this step did overlap with steps two and three to a certain extent. But I name it as the fourth step because I didn't finish with seminary until I'd already moved on from Chris and settled into my life in the Green House. Plus, the cumulative impact of all that I'd learned in my Biblical studies courses didn't quite hit me—and probably couldn't have hit me—until after I was both sufficiently angry with God and happily engaged in a lifestyle that younger, more prudish me would have been worried would get her in trouble.

For me, things needed to happen in this order: I'd set aside my fears and my subservience, and, as I was doing so, I happened to learn that I'd had nothing to be scared about or submissive to in the first place. I learned that Christianity—or Christianity as I knew it, anyway—was kind of made up.

That "as I knew it" is important here. I still wondered if there was an underlying truth to my faith—a new-to-me way of doing Christianity—that was available despite all that humans had piled on top of the religion with their own self-centered interpretations and power-grabbing theologies. At this point, I still, somehow, believed in God and wanted to find the right way of knowing Him, if there was one.

As far as the Bible was concerned, though, I was over it. Once I graduated from seminary and no longer had to read it for homework, even after so many years spent poring over its pages with inquisitiveness and adoration, I found that I was no longer interested in reading it at all. On top of that, the Episcopal church I'd started going to shortly after moving into the Green House went to the trouble of putting each week's relevant scriptural passages in the packet-length program that was handed out before each service, thus making it unnecessary for me to bring my Bible with me on Sunday mornings. Since they no longer served a purpose for me beyond their existence as sentimental objects, I left my Bibles (I'd collected a few different translations by that point) to sit untouched on my shelves, collecting dust alongside other books with which I'd shared profound experiences but would likely never crack open again.

SOME PEOPLE SAY, "Never meet your heroes." It's a warning about the possibility of disillusionment when reputation meets reality, or when the glory of accomplishment is tempered by a less than stellar personality. I've heard of folks meeting famous actors whom they idolized, only to find the stars snobby and dismissive. Or someone who met their favorite author, and the guy turned out to be brazenly sexist, even within the span of a brief interaction.

After such a disappointing encounter, you wonder what

to do with the affection and respect you'd held toward this person. Your feelings were real, and their skill is real (or so you hope), but your loyalty to them—your worship of them, even—assumed too much about their character. You find yourself in a conundrum: Do you continue to sing their praises, despite finding out that they're not the kind of person you'd want to associate with in real life? Or do you choose to let go of an image that had provided you with hope and inspiration for who knows how many years?

For evangelical Christians, studying the Bible in-depth can be a bit like meeting a hero and the encounter not going so well. Perhaps that's why so many avoid it. It's a gut-wrenching process, for sure. But I think it's a good one, too. It's important to know what you're really staking your life on. And if the timing of this process in your life allows you to go into it when you are becoming—or maybe even already are—somewhat disillusioned with the Christianity that you grew up with, which was the case for me, my guess is that you'll likely be more open to accepting the truth that things aren't as self-evident as you'd been led to believe.

Then again, maybe—unlike me—after a thorough, historical-critical study of the Bible, your theology doesn't really change. Maybe you still view scripture and God in basically the same way, despite the questions that have been raised. If that's what happens for you, great. To each their own. Whatever makes you feel free. But at least you have all the facts. Now, at least you know that you are making an informed choice, and that the choice is yours.

The most important thing, however, is that your examination of the Bible involves learning *about* the book, not just reading it over and over again and talking about it with friends who already believe basically the same things that you do. I thought I really knew the text because I'd made the words a part of me. When tested on my knowledge of what was printed on the page, I could pass with flying colors. Yet I was still ignorant. So when I say "study the Bible" for your fourth step, I don't mean that kind of studying—the kind of studying you do for a test, reading a document over and over again with the intention of infusing your mind and body with its language. I don't mean make the Bible a part of you.

I mean, in fact, quite the opposite. I mean study the text as a scientist, as a critic. Study it, if you can, like a nonbeliever. Learn about where it was written, when it was written, by whom it was written, and what else was written that a bunch of powerful men in an exclusive meeting decided would not be a part of the canon. All of these things should make a difference to one's faith, and realizing them helps one understand that the claim that Christianity is the one true path to salvation is based on a concerning number of contingencies.

Of course, not everyone can go to seminary. Not everyone wants to, and not everyone should. But getting an accredited degree that involves Biblical studies classes isn't the only way to learn about the Bible. There are libraries. There's the internet. Read widely. Go online and see if you can find syllabi for Biblical studies classes at institutions that have a reputation for taking a more critical approach, and then use those as a starting point for your research. If you have friends who did go to seminary, ask if you can borrow their books, and then ask if you can talk about what you find. Compare opinions. Really get to know what people are saying about this text that you love, that you've based your whole life upon.

However you go about studying it, if you can do so with some semblance of detachment—with a willingness to learn uncomfortable truths—you will be confronted with the question of what and whom you're really putting your faith in. This question is an opportunity. Not shying away from it, which should be easier thanks to how you've embraced your doubts and your anger toward God and the acceptance and love you've found in the places the church told you to stay away from, is yet another chance to move closer to the knowledge of what you yourself believe, even if that means moving further away from the church. I wonder how you will answer.

STEP 5
KEEP YOUR EYES OPEN IN CHURCH

Of all the things I struggled with as a girl being raised in the Christian church, one aspect that proved particularly difficult for me was keeping my eyes closed when I prayed. It sounds silly, I know, but this deceptively superficial failing was truly a source of shame for me that, to my dismay, popped up on a regular basis. In fact, it's one of my earliest memories.

When I was very young and attending the Baptist elementary school where I first asked Jesus to come into my heart, there were certain religious rituals that I had to participate in daily. For instance, we were trained to pledge allegiance to both the Christian flag and the American flag every morning. If you didn't grow up with knowledge of such a thing, the Christian flag is mostly white, representing the inherent purity of Jesus as well as the sins of the believer being washed away. Then, there is a red cross in the upper left corner, contained within a blue square. The red represents Jesus' blood, of course, shed for the forgiveness of all, and the blue stands for the waters of baptism. I can no longer recite the whole pledge by heart, but I do have a clear recollection of standing for it, my right hand resting faithfully on my sternum, each school day for the better part of four years.

We also prayed in class every day. When I was in kindergarten, the group of us sat in a circle on the floor to do so. Our teacher would shepherd us students to a particular corner of the room where we gathered around, closed our eyes, bowed our heads, and shared with God whatever was on our little five-year-old hearts.

It probably sounds more somber than it was. Our teacher was a delightful woman, and I felt a great affection for her. I imagine there was a lot of love in those prayer circles. Unfortunately, the only thing I really remember about them, other than the feeling of the rough industrial carpet making itchy indents on the outsides of my legs and the fact that it was in one of those morning circles that I dutifully requested my personal salvation, is that I could never keep my eyes closed during the prayer.

I just kept peeking. I couldn't help it. No matter how hard I tried to stop my eyelids from opening, I always ended up giving in, if only for a second of relief before closing them again. I would glance around the circle at my classmates, who all seemed somehow able to keep their eyes closed the whole time, before trying—always unsuccessfully—to return to my inner self and stay there. I envied them, and I was baffled by their ability to sit in self-imposed darkness so peacefully.

Occasionally, our teacher would spy my open, wandering eyes and speak a gentle reminder to the class that everyone keep their eyes closed until the end of the prayer. It could be that there were others as antsy as I was, but I did not notice them, and I knew her admonition was never not about me. I was also never bothered by the fact that her catching me looking meant that she was looking too, focused as I was on figuring out the secret formula for controlling my face and my mind so I could do what they told me, even if my eyelids fluttered and my attention clambered desperately for the light.

The struggle continued as I got older. At no point did I develop the skill of keeping my eye closed through an entire prayer, though with time and the perspective it inevitably brings I did eventually give myself a little more grace about it. Still, when I scroll through my rolodex of church-related memories, I have a mental picture of every congregation I've ever been a part of collectively hunched in a moment of prayer around me, and each image is accompanied by a feeling of frustration with my incurable restlessness. No matter where I was or who was doing the praying, I couldn't help but steal a glance. Even now, having replaced the habit of Christian prayer with a fits-and-starts practice of Buddhist meditation, I still find the hardest part to be keeping my eyes closed.

WHEN I REFLECT on this particular, seemingly trivial obstacle that I could never quite overcome, I have to wonder why they asked us to close our eyes at all. Without fail, whether you were a child or an adult, the instruction before praying was always, "Let's bow our heads and close our eyes." Like everything else the church asked of me, I took these expectations for physical posture as a given, and while it was hard for me to follow the rule, I never questioned why I was being asked to do the thing in the first place. On the contrary, I judged myself for my inability to easily obey it, which sums up my overall relationship to Christianity quite nicely.

Now, though, having realized how important breaking free of this mundane instruction was to my own experience of leaving the church, I find myself curious about where the tradition comes from. What does closing one's eye have to do with anything? After all, these directions for prayer are not in the Bible. There are stories where Jesus talks about being mindful not to put on a show with your prayers (Matthew 6) and one spot where he shares with his disciples what words to pray after they ask him to teach them (Luke 11). Jesus himself goes off on his own to pray a whole bunch, too. But never are people described as praying with their eyes closed, nor is anybody ever explicitly instructed to do so. In fact, in the Gospel of John, it says that Jesus "looked toward heaven" as he was speaking to God shortly before his arrest and crucifixion. So, where did the practice of everyone closing their eyes during prayer originate?

One idea is that closing one's eyes, in addition to bowing one's head, is a form of reverence toward God. It's the way a person might be expected to approach a king or some other supreme ruler, and that's why, at some point, such a posture became the traditional mode of prayer in Christianity. Another theory is that, at some point in history, some Christians decided that keeping one's eyes closed during prayer was a way to avoid idol worship because one's attention would be focused, in an abstract sort of way, on the invisible, uncapturable *being* of God rather than any physical stand-in. Of course, many Christians around the world also find that looking at icons during prayer deepens the experience, so I wouldn't say that reasoning is widespread.

The other option—and the one I think might be the most common logic these days, whatever the historical roots of the practice—is the idea that keeping your eyes closed helps with concentration. When your eyes are closed, you're supposedly not distracted by the world around you, whether that's the people you're with or the objects you're surrounded by. You can just focus on the words being spoken aloud, or the ones you're saying to God quietly inside your own head, and forget about everything else for a moment. Using this reasoning, closing your eyes helps keep the mind from wandering—it allows you to be swept away, or caught up in, the moment. Unless of course you can't stop thinking about how uncomfortable it is to keep your eyes closed, but maybe that was just me.

THOUGH I WAS NEVER able to settle comfortably into self-imposed darkness during prayer, there was one activity in church where I found that I could detach from the surrounding world and get lost like they wanted me to—one part of the whole ritual where I actually chose to close my eyes, even though it wasn't expected that we do so—and that was while I was singing. The interesting thing about this is that, whereas the practice of praying with one's eyes closed was ubiquitous, even insisted upon throughout Protestant churches well before I was born, singing with one's eyes closed was not quite so traditional when I was a child.

No one told or even asked me to do it. In fact, I never even tried to do it until the church I grew up in became slightly more charismatic, around the time I was in high school. Before that, everyone had their eyes open during worship—you had to look at the hymnal, after all. (For those unfamiliar, it's common in the evangelical world to refer to the songs that are sung to God, as well as the act of singing them, as simply "worship.") Or, if you'd already sung the song enough times to memorize the melody and the words, you found some spot on the ground or the wall or maybe even the back of someone's head to awkwardly stare at until the song was done.

Then, in the 1990s—the time of my adolescence—things started to shift. A trend of so-called "seeker friendly" churches swept across the United States. It impacted congregations that hadn't been particularly evangelical in their approach before, including the one in which I was raised, and it fundamentally changed the church experience for so many, including myself.

The point of the seeker-friendly movement was to make Christianity appealing to the average, secular-minded person who wouldn't otherwise be interested in church, or who might be scared that they would feel out of place at a religious service. To this end, a lot of churches became non-denominational, in name if not in actual practice. For example, the church I grew up in removed "Baptist" from its name and replaced it with "Community," even though they remained affiliated with the Baptist denomination. Have you noticed how many "Community" churches there are out there, or how many churches you pass by that have "Bible" in the title, and thought to yourself, *Well that seems generic?* This is why.

A lot of churches—including my own—revamped their aesthetic, too. One Sunday morning when I was in middle school, I walked into my church's sanctuary to find that the dark wood beams that had hovered over me while I worshiped in my childhood had been painted a faded shade of teal. I saw that the pews and their 1970s'-orange upholstery, where I would spread my body out when the sermon got too boring and I was still small enough to do so, had been replaced with rows of individual chairs, the cushions of which matched the color of the beams above. Noticing that the sounds of my footsteps were more muffled than usual, I looked down to discover that the glossy pebbledash floor I used to stare at when I couldn't keep my eyes closed the whole way through a prayer had been covered up with carpet.

Everything looked and felt different. At the same time that I was going through the ravages of puberty, this holy space that I was so intimately familiar with, and intimidated by, became softer and lighter and more anesthetizing, like a doctor's office waiting room. I half expected to hear smooth jazz playing at a whisper over the sound system as the rest of the congregation trickled in.

Personally, I found the remodel ugly and sad. I suppose that's what everyone feels when the monuments of their childhood get refurbished or replaced. What I did end up loving about the new direction the church was heading, however, was the change in music. Things started to get a little more contemporary in the worship realm. A second service was added to the Sunday morning schedule so that those who preferred a guitar and a drum kit over organ-backed hymns could try out this new style, and those who preferred the old ways wouldn't have to suffer through rock-inspired racket while they were trying to respectfully praise their god. No one had to tell me twice that I could sleep in and still go to church, so the second service is where I ended up, and where I learned how easy it was for me to release from the surrounding world when I was singing to the Lord.

The songs we sang in that later service were written more like pop songs. Granted, for the most part, they wouldn't have been *good* pop songs, but they had structures and melodies that were closer to what we were hearing on secular radio stations, as opposed to the older style of church songs that had probably been arranged for a choir. These contemporary praise songs were simpler: They were easy to learn, easy to sing, and, consequently, easy to get lost in. They were designed for the participant to have a more emotive experience, one that was particularly conducive to being swept away by the strange, exciting power of the Holy Spirit.

Because I was a teenager when this shift in musical style happened at my church, I think I was particularly prone to getting hooked on the more emotional style of worship that the contemporary praise songs were meant to foster. I could really get into them. The experience was basically the same as the combination of comfort and thrill that flooded over me when I put on a non-church music album that spoke to me deeply, except with these songs I was also directly communicating with God, so there was this supernatural aspect on top of whatever it is about a well-wrought combination of music and lyrics that just moves you.

At some point not long after this shift in musical style happened, I noticed that certain of my fellow congregants were starting to close their eyes as we sang our worship songs during the second service on Sunday mornings. Now and then I saw a hand lifted, too, palm open toward the ceiling. At first I found the gesture to be a little corny, even embarrassing to watch. We were still far from being a truly charismatic church, after all. I was used to things being kind of stuffy. But, again, I knew the joy of shutting the world out while I sang or danced along to my favorite secular music, and the words to these new church songs were easy to remember, which meant that it only took two or three rounds of following along with the lyrics that were being projected onto the retractable screen at the front of the sanctuary before I had most of them down by heart. So, one Sunday morning I decided to try it out for myself—to lose sight of the people around me and quietly slip away into the transcendent space of my mind. When we came to a song I had memorized, I closed my eyes and did not open them again until the last chord was strummed. I had finally figured out how to let go.

It wasn't long before this became the norm for me. I'd discovered a gateway to an out-of-body experience. It was almost addictive, the relief of feeling free from a physical form that I was often disgusted by and of being released, if only for a few minutes, from my constantly shifting, visually-driven analysis of the material world that surrounded and overwhelmed me. When the instruments started playing and I closed my eyes and started singing, I could truly just focus on the feeling of my passion for God. I couldn't wait to say goodbye to everyday life for a while, and I was always a little bit sad when the music ended and I had to return to being stuck in my corporeal form. In this context, where I'd found the key to another realm of experience, I never once struggled to keep my eyes shut.

Imagining what I must have looked like when I was caught up in one of these guards-down, full-throated moments of total commitment to the moment of worship is a bit embarrassing, to be honest. I was a cliche, not far from the oh-so-mockable images of a TV preacher's audience swept up in a moment of rapture that's simultaneously collective and private, and thus hard to watch. If I was really in the zone, my eyes weren't just closed, they were clenched. When it came to my hands, any onlooker would be able to tell just how much I was feeling a song by whether neither, one, or both were raised. The height of the raise was telling, too: The higher the hand, the louder I was singing. During particularly slow or somber moments, my head was likely bowed, whereas when things really picked up and became either joyous or loud, I tilted my face up to heaven like I was enjoying a refreshing spring rain or a warm beam of sun. Sometimes, I wept as I sang to my Lord.

I spent years like this, allowing my soul to free-fall into a euphoric, sometimes ecstatic abyss of pure emotion during musical worship. If it wasn't during Sunday morning services, then it was during midweek youth group gatherings, or, once

I got to college, impromptu evening huddles in a campus courtyard to which someone just happened to bring an acoustic guitar. This was how I learned to really detach from the concrete, rational world in church—to release my grip on external input, to hit pause on my thinking mind and be consumed by the presence of God (or what felt like the presence of God) for a while.

It's also what the grown-ups were always getting at, I think, when they insisted that we close our eyes during prayer. Perhaps not the bliss I felt when I sang my love to God with my whole heart—that bar was quite high—but the self-surrendering trust in the ways of the church that totally losing oneself in a moment of worship created. The giving up of a vantage point of appraisal and control and allowing oneself to be led by the Lord, or whoever purported to be working in His stead at that moment. They wanted me to yield, and I'd learned how.

IT COULD HAVE GONE on this way for the rest of my life, I suppose. I might have returned again and again until my dying day to the rituals I knew would give me a chance to push pause, at least once a week, on the exhausting hypervigilance that was my natural state. I could easily have kept using the church, and specifically the way I got to sing when I was at church, as my transport to euphoria. But there were certain events—that dreadful break-up, the opportunity to move into the Green House, and my encounters with critical Biblical study, to name a few—that brought me to a crossroads in my faith as I entered adulthood. And at those crossroads I chose, whether consciously or unintentionally—perhaps sometimes a little of both—to take up directions in my life that led me further away from the church instead of deeper into it.

You know the stories of those choices by now, so I won't revisit them in detail here. The point is that, by the time I was in my late twenties and nearing the end of my time in seminary, the cumulative effect of all those experiences, of all the doubt and anger and disillusionment, was that I did not find church to be a very safe space anymore. All my life, they'd asked me to close my eyes and trust them, to put aside my reasoning brain and slip into an immaterial dimension where I could feel myself communing with a deity who was supposedly pure love. And yet, they themselves withheld love. They'd asked me to let go of skepticism, but all the while they weren't telling me the whole truth. They weren't being forthright with me—about sin, about consequences, about the history of our religion. About, it seemed, any of it.

The more obvious their disingenuousness became to me, the less I felt like I could stomach Sunday mornings as I'd known them. The exhilaration brought on by worship that I'd been experiencing since I was a teenager was getting harder and harder to access, and the tighter I closed my eyes, the more frustrating the situation became. I needed a change. But yet again, as pathetic as it may sound, I still wasn't ready to leave church behind for good. Even this far into my trek beyond the bounds of the Christianity I grew up with, I was still a believer—in the existence of God and the teachings of Jesus, if nothing else. I just wanted to do church differently than what I was used to, even if I wasn't sure what exactly that meant or looked like.

It was while I was in this state of religious discontent, groping for some last-ditch handhold by which I might continue to cling to Christianity, that my housemate invited me to go with him to visit the Episcopal church down the street. In addition to its reputation for being progressive in its theology, which was something that was especially appealing to me after I'd learned my lesson about how little the conservative church I was raised in actually knew about the people they deemed sinners, I was also interested in trying out a milder and more mindful style of worship. I was hopeful that participating in an open-eyed, liturgical tradition—an approach to church that I'd grown familiar with during the semester I spent studying in England, attending Anglican services nearly every week I was there—might be just what I needed to get away from all the drama of the evangelicals. My hope turned out to be well-placed. But what I didn't realize was how the very thing that made Anglicanism so appealing at this stage in my journey—namely, a style of worship grounded in the material world and lacking the addictive quality of hyper-emotionalism—would also be the very thing that revealed to me how irrecoverable my once-zealous relationship with the church really was.

PUT SIMPLY, a liturgical church is one that follows a set worship practice, both weekly and yearly. So, for example, whether you attend the Catholic Church, the Episcopal Church, or a Lutheran congregation, on any given Sunday you can expect basically the same routine as all the other Sundays, often involving a processional, prayers, scripture readings, songs, a short sermon, the eucharist—what I grew up referring to as "communion"—and a recessional. In addition to that, over the course of the year, liturgical churches follow a schedule that determines which bits of scripture and which prayers are said on that particular week in the church's year-long calendar.

These are also the types of churches that call for a lot of physical participation. Usually the congregation is asked to stand during certain parts of the service, to kneel during others, and to walk to the front of the sanctuary to receive the bread and the wine that represent (or, depending on your theology, actually are) Jesus' body and blood, sacrificed for all for the forgiveness of sins.

Interestingly, despite all this choreography, I don't remember ever being asked to close my eyes during a liturgical service. After all, since the language of the prayers was predetermined and often included a scripted call-and-response that's printed out and handed to each congregant as they enter the church, for folks who are sighted, keeping one's eyes closed would tend to inhibit the ability to participate. Plus, these types of churches are often very beautiful to look at from the inside: colorful stained glass, delicate woodwork, soaring ceilings accented with graceful chandeliers. No wonder they never asked people to keep themselves in the dark—there was too much magnificence to take in.

I know a lot of people who find the liturgical style to be stale. I can understand that. There is quite a bit of repetition, not just in any one service but across the weeks and years. Perhaps there is a risk that meaning will be lost in the routine. There's also little room for improvisation—maybe Americans especially feel their self-expression a little hampered by such an approach. For me, though, when I first encountered Anglicanism during the autumn I spent in England as a senior in college, I found myself comforted by the rhythm of the liturgy. Despite the fact that I was still in the midst of my honeymoon phase with the 'contemporary' evangelical worship style, I discovered that something inside me felt at home in a church that was more focused on a collective ritual of reverence than the fostering of private, individualized conversations with the Lord.

Who knows—maybe I just liked that it was novel. But even if that was the case, I'm grateful that I was introduced to a liturgical style way back then, because by the time I was down in Southern California, feeling mad at God and suspicious of the church and unable to stomach yet another nondenominational worship leader asking me to close my eyes and sing to Jesus like he was the love of my life, I remembered how I'd loved the artistry and communal ceremony of the Anglican churches so many years prior, and I knew to say yes when I was invited to attend a service that would end up changing my life.

What a surprise and a relief that Episcopal church in Pasadena was. The visual beauty was all there, of course. And, as I mentioned earlier, I was taken aback—in a good way—by the church's stance on all the issues that had been quietly bugging me for so many years about the Christianity with which I was familiar. This church was proudly celebratory of its LGBTQIA+ members, used "she" and "he" interchangeably when referring to God, and seemed to focus almost entirely on helping people live in safety and freedom and love in this life, on this planet, as opposed to fixating on the destination of everyone's eternal souls.

On top of all that, there was, as I had been longing for, the very deliberate and formal ritual of the weekly service—at least, it felt deliberate and formal compared to the tradition I was accustomed to and trying to break free from. Sure, my little Baptist congregation and those like it that I tried out when I moved to Pasadena had their routines and observances, but they were all so focused on the internal experience, and my internal experience was no longer matching up with what the church wanted from me. These Episcopal services, on the other hand, just like the Anglican ones I'd visited in college, seemed to be much more about what the group was doing, and being aware of what the group was doing, and working together to celebrate God.

What I discovered, almost immediately upon visiting, was that all the standing and sitting and kneeling and standing again, reading prayers together, and walking with each other to the front of the church to receive the eucharist from the hands of the priests captured my attention in a way that still allowed me to think about why we were all there. It was a very conscious worship practice. I found that I was able to participate in something that felt important, to feel acceptance and belonging, without getting swept away. My body felt grounded, and I was allowed, quite literally, to see what was going on.

I was so relieved by my experience at this church that I managed to stay for a few years. And I didn't just stay—I got involved. I can't remember if it was through mutual friends or a chance encounter, but I somehow found out about a social group within the church that catered to mostly childless folks in their 20s and 30s. It's not that people with children were not welcome; it's just that they generally gravitated toward the family ministries, and so the makeup of this group was the result of a kind of natural sifting process. We all bonded because we didn't necessarily fit in elsewhere in the church's typical nuclear family-oriented setting.

It had been a long time since I'd felt like I clicked at a church. I'd become too disillusioned to feel comfortable being my whole, honest self in any evangelical community. So when I found this group at the Episcopal church, I felt like I'd discovered the people who were exactly right for that moment. I found commiseration with others who'd grown up in conservative traditions and wanted to be free of the pressure and the shame but still wanted to be able to be part of a church. I found a group of people who were the opposite of puritanical. On the contrary, many of these folks were living in ways that looked a lot like what the church I grew up in called sin. Yet, as with the friends I gained when I moved into the Green House, they were also generally pretty happy, and they'd found a place where they could be affirmed as unconditionally loved children of God without having to change behavior they didn't believe was wrong.

I was so excited to have come across this church where I actually fit in that I jumped at the chance to be on the group's leadership team when I was asked. Even writing this now, over a decade later, I'm stunned that I actually wanted to participate at that level. I am not what you would call a "joiner." But the craving I'd had to return to the depth of camaraderie that church had provided me in my youth must have been quite strong. The deeper I got into the community, the more it became my home away from home, and the more confident I felt in embracing it. I was totally supported; my skeptical, jaded perspective was honored, and I felt safe and comfortable enough to start giving back.

IN THE MOMENT, I thought my issues with Christianity were more or less solved. I thought I'd found a way to be integrated into church, and have church integrated into me, despite all the faith that I'd left behind—or that had been stripped away from me—by that point. But, as with everything in life, what was at first pleasantly surprising sooner or later became normalized. After a couple of years of enthusiastic participation, once I'd finished seminary and started working full time, my life became too busy for me to stay totally committed to my role on the young adult group's leadership team. I decided to step away from that position, and though I continued to participate in social events, eventually I found myself less invested in the community than I once was.

Around the same time, after having found peace and comfort in the whole-bodied, open-eyed worship style of the Episcopalians for a good while, my attention began to drift during services. My sight, which I was finally free to use, started wandering from the splendor of the building and the words of the liturgy printed out for us each week and settled instead on the folks around me. I started watching us—not individual people, but the movement of the collective—with a more disinterested eye. I started thinking about that movement, and started to wonder whether, despite how liberal the church was in its stated beliefs, all of the standing and the kneeling actually implied something more traditional and more oppressive in terms of our relationship with God.

Once I started thinking about that, I couldn't stop. First, I realized that the kneeling posture must have come out of a theology that sees God as a king—*the* king, really. (That theory is also used by some historians to explain the tradition of closing one's eyes during prayer.) Then I started thinking about how a monarchy is not a particularly progressive way of envisioning a religion, even as a metaphor. Yes, it's a prevalent image in the Bible, but there are lots of social systems present in (and not questioned by) the Bible that are no longer considered acceptable even in so-called Christian societies. Tradition did not seem like a good enough reason to buy into a version of God that, from my perspective at least, necessitated unquestioning submission to His—or even Her—authority.

There was so much supposedly Bible-based theology that this church was turning on its head, so many well-established rules that it was changing or refusing to support because it prioritized love over dogma, and yet—it dawned on me thanks to the invitation to keep my eyes open through everything—that we all continued to kneel in prayer as if God was our monarch despite the authoritarianism baked into that analogy. Slowly, I realized that, for me, referring to God as "She" now and then wasn't enough to balance out the eager genuflection that we all engaged in every week.

This was not the revelation I'd been looking for. I didn't want to have a reason to disapprove of this institution that had been such a safe space for me right when I needed it. I was disheartened to see that, despite how much I'd gained from this fellowship, I was back in the very situation I thought I'd managed to escape: habitually deferring to a deity who'd proved to be unreliable, just because everyone else was doing it and always had. Just because I was supposed to.

I started to sense a resistance rising up in me every Sunday morning as I watched the congregation go through its motions all around me like a current I could either relax into or determine to swim against. I questioned whether I could, in good conscience, continue to participate in all the kneeling now that I'd had an epiphany about what that gesture was really saying about my relationship to God.

I also wondered if I was overthinking it. What was the harm in going with the flow, especially when so much was right about this church? Couldn't I just go through the motions without needing everything to be a perfect metaphor? After all, leaving that congregation would mean losing community—again. More than that, it would mean that I'd come to the end of my rope: there were no more options left if I wanted to stay within the faith. If I couldn't remain invested in this church, of all churches, what choice was left for me in terms of finding a version of Christianity that I could get behind?

The stakes were high enough that I didn't want to leave on a whim, even if I was growing increasingly uncomfortable. So, once my resistance to the collective obeisance kicked in, I decided to try some calculated non-participation. Banking on that church's own claim that there was no real obligation to take a particular pose during prayer (the liturgical instructions we read each Sunday instructed congregants to kneel or stand "if able"), I sat back while most of the people around me pulled down the kneelers in front of their pews and lowered themselves onto their bent legs, just inches off the floor.

It felt a little strange, knowing that I was doing this not out of any physical limitation but simply because I was not feeling good about the morality of the action. Still, I needed to see whether it was possible for me to find a happy medium that allowed me to opt out of what made me uncomfortable while still being able to enjoy all that I loved about the church, including the fact that this was a place where I felt like I could do my own thing for my own reasons and not be judged for it—yet another reason why I was hoping I wouldn't have to give the place up.

For better or worse, I was able to stay in those pews, not kneeling but not walking out either, for a little while longer. Watching the congregation join in worship around me, and in some ways wishing that I too could join in without such an unrelenting awareness of all the problems I had with what our words and actions implied, I felt so grateful for all that this particular church had given me. At the same time, I wondered how long I could last in this limbo. How badly did I want church? How badly did I need it? I was afraid to open myself up to the truth, but I was also becoming even more terrified by the prospect of a future spent suppressing my discomfort and objections.

U<small>LTIMATELY</small>, that Episcopal church was the last congregation I was a part of before I stopped going to church altogether. Though some part of me knew that I was nearing the end of my time in Christianity, my last Sunday there wouldn't come for a while longer. There were still a couple more steps necessary to get me to the point where I was ready to say goodbye for good. But even without having yet reached that precipice, it was the freedom I had to open my eyes, and what I found when I did, that brought me closer than I'd ever been to the edge of a new life.

When I was welcomed to pray and worship with eyes open, I was able to—maybe even compelled to—acknowledge what we were all doing together there in that gorgeous building. I was able to see how that lovely space, while it housed some relatively open minds and looked quite different on the surface from the churches I'd grown up in, still represented the same religion and housed many of the same beliefs I had been struggling to stomach in other iterations of the faith. It was still Christianity. And Christianity, I was so close to realizing, was the thing I no longer wanted.

This is what I would recommend for those who find themselves where I was right before this step, detaching from religion but also not wanting to let it go: Keep your eyes open in church. The whole time. Or, if it applies to the type of denomination you're a part of, try staying seated when everyone else is kneeling or standing. The goal is to identify the tactics that your congregation uses to create an experience, whether it's individual or collective, where the grounded, rational world is abandoned in favor of transcendence, or even just the comfort of going with the flow of a collective tradition.

To be clear, transcendence is not a bad thing. Nor are traditions, especially those that belong to and sustain whole communities. But when you're trying to question the nature of the tradition itself, or the institution to which it belongs, it's all too easy to get stalled in that interrogation if you keep caving to the pressure to melt all the way into the moment and leave your worries behind. Instead, consider how you can free yourself up to be able to come at things from another angle—one that's both curious and critical.

I also want to stay wary of the implication that lacking physical sight is a bad thing in and of itself. Being blind or having low vision doesn't mean that a person is inherently more vulnerable to deception or manipulation. Nevertheless, blindness is often used as a metaphor for ignorance, and "seeing" is a common figure of speech for having or gaining true knowledge and insight. The Bible itself uses this metaphor regularly, and the analogy between blindness/sight and ignorance/revelation has carried through the church's language since then. (Think of the lyrics to "Amazing Grace," a song well known even outside of Christianity: "I once was lost/but now I'm found/was blind, but now I see.") These ways of speaking get into our brain and bury themselves deep in our subconscious, and we erroneously believe that we must physically see the world in order to truly know it.

My aim here is not to equate seeing with knowing, but to call out the methods that the church uses to disconnect its members from their perception of the outside world so that they can engage in communication with an invisible God no matter what others (or even they themselves, in moments of greater clarity) might think about it. In my experience, having everyone close their eyes, through either explicit or implicit instruction, was one of the more effective methods used. Of course, it worked because the majority of people were sighted, and we live in a very visually oriented society, so pushing pause on that aspect of sensory input was an expedient way for most people to detach from one thing that anchored them to this mundane existence and let their inner selves sail into a place free of judgment and rationality.

But the church could use any other mode of sensory deprivation and I would still balk against it. The point isn't *seeing* in particular—the point is to cling to one's embodiedness in that setting. To refuse to be swept away, no matter how much you are aching for it, no matter how nice a break from the worries of the world it would be. For me, that meant keeping my eyes open, which the Episcopal tradition gave me a chance to do. Then, that led me to realizing how my whole body was going through motions that my heart and mind couldn't get behind anymore. I needed to enhance rather than dull my perception of what we were doing in those church buildings in order to come to that realization.

Given what I learned from these experiences, I recommend doing a careful examination of what's happening around you during church if you can. Not without love, but definitely without normalizing. Whatever measures you're in the habit of using to move yourself into a space of pure emotion, refrain from them. Instead, think about the scene taking place around you. Watch the way people move—sitting, standing, or kneeling as one. Watch as people raise their hands toward the ceiling as if their straining fingers were actually capable of touching the edge of God. Or just watch as they stand stiffly.

Hear, too, the words that are being used about how humans relate to God. Do you agree with them? Think about how God is gendered in your church, or referred to as a political authority—for example, as a king. Step out of feeling mode for at least one Sunday morning. Be a visitor, even if you are technically a member. Detach, so you can truly know what you are doing when you're there.

If, after that, you're still into church and all the rituals it contains—if it's what you want to be doing with your body, mind, and time—then great. Keep going. But if it starts to seem silly to you—if you would truly rather be doing something else; if you are getting to the point where you just can't stand to act as if you are the glad subject of a royal ruler, or you are fed up with having to argue yourself into participating in this religion every Sunday—then don't automatically dismiss those gravitations.

Break the spell. Allow church to be a grounded reality. Get it out of the ether and back into the physically perceivable world. This is where it is taking place, after all. And this is where you will be able to know, with something approaching confidence, whether your journey has taken you to the point where you are not quite past belief—that step will come soon enough—but you are most definitely done with any kind of self-denying worship.

STEP 6
ASK THE BIG QUESTIONS

I remember quite vividly the moment the first question came to me. I was sitting on the porch of the Green House, in one of the two molded plastic Adirondack chairs that a housemate had picked up from a discount grocery store a few blocks up the road when we first moved in.

It was a warm, sunny day—the kind of day you picture when you think of Southern California. I'd gone out to the porch to read and enjoy the weather, but I couldn't focus. My eyes kept straying from whatever book I'd brought out there with me to the tree that grew from the very center of the front lawn. It was full and healthy, though probably in need of a trim, with broad green leaves that glowed when the sun's light came through from above.

As I looked up at the luminous leaves, I noticed an unusual energy coming from within me, the same way the tree seemed lit from within when the sun was behind it. It wasn't a frantic or anxious energy—those I was familiar with —but an uncanny sense of power, radiating from my core.

And not a power over anything, not a feeling of dominance, but a strange, sudden knowing that I could trust myself, that I was good and smart and capable of doing what I wanted with my own life.

It was a happy feeling, and while I was thinking about where it might have come from, a question popped into my head—a question that I think had been forming in me for some time, but I wasn't ready to ask it of myself until this moment. Or, I wasn't ready to answer it. Not until that day, on that porch, as I stared at the leaves, after years of weathering doubts and despair and disillusionment and the slow detachment from the religion I'd used to define myself up until that point.

The question was, *What if Jesus was not God?* A stunning proposition for someone with my history, but one that, apparently, it was time for me to consider. And one that immediately reminded me of a theological teaching I'd encountered several times throughout my youth.

Those who grew up in Christianity, especially an evangelical version, will likely be familiar with C. S. Lewis's trilemma. You might not know it by that name (I didn't, until I started doing research for this book), but you'll surely be familiar with the idea. In the mid-1900s, Lewis, who was a Belfast-born author and scholar—and, interestingly, a former atheist—laid out an argument in support of the claim that it's unreasonable for a person to simply embrace Jesus as an admirable teacher and ignore the Christianity of it all. He contended, in other words, that you can't say that Jesus was a good man of history and at the same time refuse to believe he was the son of God because there is an internal contradiction in that position.

According to Lewis's reasoning—which was, by the way, put forth by a number of preachers and theologians before him, though he's most famous for it now—if we take into consideration all of the things Jesus said that are written down in the Gospels, he had to be either a "lunatic" (to use Lewis's word), a con man, or actually the son of God. He could not, however, be both exemplary and not divine, because he claimed divinity. To take away the aspect of divinity would mean that he was either a "madman" (again, Lewis's word) who only *thought* he was the son of God, or he was intentionally deceiving people by saying he was the son of God even though it wasn't true. In either case, what kind of moral mentor could he be? According to Lewis, this leaves us only one choice: to embrace Jesus as our savior, or to reject him outright.

Someone at some point boiled this argument down to a catchy alliteration that generations of church kids across the country have had drilled into their brains by every pastor and preacher they've encountered in their lifetimes—Jesus was either a lunatic, a liar, or Lord. And we were convinced that this was an airtight argument, an actual reason to think Jesus' divinity was undeniable and that becoming a Christian was indeed the only way to get into heaven (or avoid hell, depending on how you were looking at it).

As for me, I understood Lewis' premises, but I never looked too closely at them. I was unable, or unwilling, to see the argument for what it was: far too simple. Maybe this analysis would be obvious to anyone not already deeply invested in Christianity as the one true way, but such was my life, knowing nothing but religious exclusivism since I came into the world. In any case, before I began my journey away from the church, I would not have presumed to push back against an idea that was presented as all but scripture. Thus, I never thought to consider, for instance, whether it was really that easy to be so sure about what exactly Jesus meant when he referred to God as his father or claimed to be the messiah. After all, there are also verses in the Gospels where Jesus appears to reject the idea that he is (or is like) God.

It wasn't until I really studied the Bible, historical contexts and all, that I developed both the knowledge and the courage to notice the problem with the fact that the only source for Jesus' teachings that Lewis's argument relies on is the Bible. This became an issue. The Bible, as I'd come to learn in seminary, is not exactly cut and dried as far as historical records go. First, as I mentioned before, there are the writings about Jesus' life that didn't make it into the canon. Might their narratives change the way we understand how he thought about his own God-ness? And what about the fact that each of the four canonical gospels is a little bit different from the others, sometimes in ways that, at least on the surface, appear contradictory? Then there are the four people who wrote the gospels that made it into the canon. They were just humans. They missed stuff; they had their biases. They had their own fears and dreams attached to the stories they were telling and hoping to share with their world. How could we not acknowledge the idea that these things might have had an impact on the words they wrote that the church now asks us to take as unedited facts?

Still, these issues were not what I was thinking of when I found myself asking that big question that day on the porch in Pasadena. What occurred to me on that day was the fact that I'd never seriously considered the first two options that Lewis presented: that Jesus of Nazareth might have been just a human man living with delusions, or that he might have been a crook. Of course, in either case, the issue of the reliability of the Bible still comes into play, since the Gospel authors all wrote about Jesus rising from the dead after his crucifixion. Even so, what I was focused on that day was how I'd managed to avoid truly engaging with all the possibilities that Lewis presented, and how I'd managed to do it for so long.

FOR YEARS, I jumped to the conclusion that Jesus was Lord without ever doing my own thinking about it. Like with so much else that the church handed to me, it happened because I paid more attention to the tone of delivery than the options with which I was presented or the logic at their core. I was focused on how things were being said, carefully picking up on the implications of what was expected of me and what was taboo, because I wanted to do right by the church. I wanted to obey. And when it came to the lunatic, liar, or Lord issue, the tone was a stern and condescending implication that the only real choice in this situation was the last one. So I never gave any weight to the other options, because they were presented to me with an attitude that insisted they weren't really choices at all.

It makes me think of how I never actually considered the point of view of my non-Christian friends when I was trying to argue them into believers back in high school. It never even occurred to me that I should. I was operating under the assumption that I already knew the truth. I had already decided what my stance was, and it was others who needed to change their minds. I came in bad faith to every argument that presented an alternative to my worldview—not out of any conscious desire to manipulate or demean those around me, but because I couldn't see my own indoctrination for what it was. There was no space, at least in my mind and in the Christianity I knew, for honestly considering another side.

It's important to take a moment to consider why that was the case. First, I felt compelled to evangelize. The church told me that it was my responsibility to save my friends' souls, that they would go to hell if they didn't believe what I believed, so I was desperate to get them on my side. On top of that, Christianity was my thing back in high school. I mean, it was my thing in college and grad school, too, but as a teenager, my faith made me unique, made me feel special—ironically, like a little bit of a rebel. No one gets through adolescence without a mask on. Often, we wear several. And we cling to them like they are our survival, because they are. For me, Christianity was not just about the salvation of my soul; it was the thing I chose to get me by, to fit me in, to usher me through life. I wasn't committed to Jesus because I'd considered all options equally and found Christianity to be the truest. It was simply what I knew, and where I felt I belonged, and a way to feel like I was doing something right and rewardable in an otherwise overwhelming life.

That need for it left me no option but to dismiss any argument against it. I always thought I was doing so because Christianity really did make the most sense. Thanks to clever-sounding rationalizations from intellectuals like Lewis, I knew how to spin something that looked and sounded like a defense of my faith. In reality, though, even if I wasn't conscious of it at the time, my motivation was my own security, not the pursuit of the truth. My faith wasn't something I felt like I had the option of giving up, and that kept me from being able to sincerely wonder whether what I'd been taught my whole life about the nature of the universe was a lie.

Thankfully, life has a way of helping us question the narratives we grew up with, if we let it. Circumstances that are painful and beyond our control offer the opportunity to consider whether the way we've been taught to approach the world is really the most helpful and healthy. Specific events don't even have to happen to us personally. If we are attentive to the stories of others and the state of our planet, we may be challenged to wonder if things are really as simple as we've always been told. For instance, a Christian as devout as I was might read the news and struggle to understand how the God she believes in can be both all-powerful and all good. This is another big question to ask, and it must be asked seriously.

As for me, the circumstances of my life, plus my reactions to them, led me to that porch one sunny day in my late twenties. In that moment, staring into those glowing leaves, pondering Jesus' divinity and recollecting Lewis' trilemma, I realized there were other questions I needed to ask myself, and that I needed to ask them with all sincerity: What if Jesus really was just a man who was delusional, or what if he was an actual liar?

Then and there, I saw how I had never truly wondered about those things before. But also, and more importantly, it dawned on me that those two options—the ones I'd always dismissed so cavalierly before—were just as, if not more, likely to be true than the conclusion that Jesus was Lord. This idea might seem obvious for some; for me, it was a revelation.

PEOPLE WHO DON'T GROW up in Christianity are often under the impression that those who buy into it wholeheartedly are unintelligent or uneducated. I can see why. In a society that prides itself on scientific advancement and linear thinking, there are a lot of aspects of the religion that come off as foolish. For example, given all the evidence we have that the universe is more than ten billion years old, how could anyone maintain a sincere belief that God created it in six days just a few thousand years ago? Committing to such a belief would seem to take either profound ignorance or a total inability to understand the facts.

Even for those Christians who aren't quite that fundamentalist, just believing in the most basic narrative—that there was once this man, born of a virgin because his father was God, who was killed and miraculously rose from the dead, and if you agree to follow his rules you will get to live with him in paradise forever, but if you choose not to he'll send you to be tortured for eternity—comes off as ludicrous. There's no proof that any of this is true. If anything, it seems to go against all probability based on what we continue to observe about the way the world works.

Personally, I never really bought into the young-earth theories thanks to relatively open-minded parents and a decent public-school education. But I did believe secret things were going on in the spiritual realm, just beyond my perception, all the time. I believed in a being that was the God of the universe, somehow both ineffable and knowable by each person on Earth. I believed that Jesus rose from the dead, and that his sacrifice made up for my sins. I believed that without accepting Jesus' death and resurrection as both true and necessary, I or anyone else would end up permanently rejected by God. And, I believed that all of this was the purest version of love.

I believed all of these things for a long time, without ever really questioning them. However, I was neither unintelligent nor uneducated. I was a star student, actually. I had nearly straight A's through high school, college, and grad school, sneaking in just one B at each level for good measure. If there was one thing that other people saw me as other than Christian—if there was any other identity I felt compelled to fulfill—it was "smart." Of course, being smart and being able to perform well in school are not necessarily the same thing. But a dearth of book smarts is usually what people are referring to when they accuse devout Christians or other religious fanatics of lacking intelligence, and that simply wasn't true for me.

I wasn't exactly uneducated, either. Sure, my elementary and secondary years weren't especially rigorous if you're going to compare them to competitive private schooling. And it's true that I did go to a Baptist church school from kindergarten through third grade. But I also read early and extensively, and I grew up in a household where staying informed and seeing the world were both high priorities. Plus, my college classes were actually quite grueling at times. The institution might have been evangelical in its beliefs, but it prided itself on providing tough and exacting scholarship. So, I didn't get less of an education than the average person. On the contrary, I imagine I got more.

And yet still, there I was, in my late twenties, only just in that moment realizing that I'd never truly considered whether Christianity was wrong. It wasn't because I was not smart, or because I hadn't ever learned anything about the world beyond my religion. It was because Christianity was a habit—a habit that I learned when I was very young, before I had the capacity to realize that it was something being handed to me, something I could choose to accept or reject.

It was my second nature. It rooted itself in the parts of my psyche that had been there since I was born, and the rest of my brain grew around it. It was already in place as I developed and matured, so the beliefs I'd been taught before my self-awareness kicked in felt natural and normal. Inherent, even. But they weren't inherent, and technically, I did have a choice. It's just that making that choice—not even making the choice to reject Christianity but just to earnestly question it—would mean disturbing the peace in the deep parts of my mind. It would mean risking the integrity of the very foundation of my self. If I pulled on those roots, what would get shaken? And if I removed them entirely, what would crumble? Would I still be there? These are not questions of intelligence or education, but of survival.

Looking for proof of God, parsing the supposed logic of apologists like Lewis, noting the dissonance between the religious narrative in my mind and what was actually transpiring in the world around me—all of these are smart, rational, perhaps even self-evident reactions to being asked to commit one's life to believing and defending any version of Christianity, especially the evangelical one that I grew up with. They are probably where any reasonable person would start. But my reluctance, or inability, to respond to the church in such a way was not for lack of intellectual acumen. It was because the church had me.

Indeed, the church had me good. It was my community; it was my purpose. It was what I was, what *we* were—my family, and the fellow believers with whom I spent most of my time outside of school. Up until my late twenties, I was willing to give up the rationality and open-mindedness that others might see as basic intelligence in order to maintain the equilibrium I'd always known, because I needed to stay comfortably in the arms of evangelicalism. I had my reasons, but they were emotional ones, which meant that it wasn't until I knew I could be safe outside of Christianity—and until I started feeling sufficiently uncomfortable within it—that true inquiry into my beliefs was possible. At that point, all of my intelligence and all of my education finally became useful for interrogating my religious commitments, but not until then.

As I said earlier, the first question to pop into my mind as I sat on the porch and admired that glowing canopy of leaves over the front yard of my perfectly imperfect home was whether Jesus was actually God. That initial question led me to thinking about Lewis' trilemma, which then brought me to the point where I had to ask myself why it couldn't be just as likely that Jesus was either intentionally lying his head off or was speaking out of a delusion.

I sat with these propositions for a while, pondering them, feeling them out. I turned them over and over in my mind, thinking about them logically. And since I'm a person who's naturally inclined to consult my intuition in all matters of deep significance, I also used my heart. It was when I brought the queries to my heart—when I swished them around in the deepest, truest part of myself like a sommelier examining an old but unfamiliar wine—that I discovered I needed to ask myself yet another, even more probing question: What do *I* believe?

You see, I couldn't tell. I couldn't tell the difference between what I thought I should believe—what I thought I needed to believe—and what I really did believe on my own. All my life, whether because of innate personality or coping skills I picked up along the way (and probably some combination of both), I'd focused on what I should do. How I should behave. I ignored my own inclinations, seeking out and clinging hard to whoever or whatever could give me some sort of sense of rightness. I wanted to know, always, that I'd done the best job that I possibly could. I needed someone to tell me what I had to do to be good.

Which is how I found myself at nearly thirty years old only just discovering that I didn't actually have any personal conviction, at my core, that the Christian story was true. There were truths in it, of course. I was all for the radical generosity, the breaking down of barriers between people, and the redemption that are in the gospel stories. But did I, Grete Howland, sincerely believe that Jesus of Nazareth was in some way literally God?

No. Not if I was being honest with myself.

In fact, I didn't even find in my heart a sincere belief that God existed at all.

That last bit took me by surprise—not the lack of belief itself, but how good it felt to finally discover that that was the case. It was like I was meeting myself for the first time. For years, I'd been so outward-oriented, so entangled in and hypnotized by the church's teachings about my own inherently corrupt notions and desires, that I was completely unfamiliar with who I really was, and I hadn't been particularly interested in finding out. I'd been unable to approach myself without prejudice, taking on other's beliefs as my own so that I could get through life knowing that I was doing alright. To suddenly be able to distinguish between what I'd been told was true and what actually made sense and felt true to me was a beautiful breakthrough.

It was also perplexing, because I couldn't pinpoint the moment at which my beliefs changed. In fact, as I go through the process of writing my story and find myself unable to locate the exact spot where I flipped sides or lost my faith, I sometimes wonder whether I ever believed at all. This is a common rebuttal used against those of us former evangelicals and former Christians who speak openly about our decision to leave either that particular version of church or church altogether. Current believers who are scandalized by such a thing tend to insist that we never had faith in the first place. For years, I joined my fellow apostles-turned-apostates in scoffing at the accusation. I knew I hadn't been faking it, that what I felt all those years was real. Once I started really digging into the details of my journey and reflecting on this step in particular, though, I started to worry that the allegation wasn't as far-fetched or presumptuous as I'd declared it to be. I hadn't been trying to deceive anyone around me with my all-out commitment to evangelicalism, but perhaps I'd been deceiving myself the whole time. Could it be true?

If all I can speak from is my experience, despite my deeply ingrained tendency to doubt said experience—a tendency that perhaps those scandalized Christians are counting on when they make such accusations—the idea that my belief was a sham doesn't make a whole lot of sense. My faith was everything to me, for as long as I could remember. Before adolescence and its awful, accompanying self-awareness kicked in, I would have told you that there was a God and Jesus was his son because I simply didn't know any different. Like a kid who believes in Santa Claus before the real world comes knocking, I would have been reciting the only narrative I'd ever been told. But I was committed. Then, once I was old enough to start forming an identity, I actively and sincerely chose the church. I know I did. Granted, there weren't a whole lot of options presented to me, but something in me—everything in me, ultimately—did choose to embrace this religion.

Even assuming that my faith was and always had been real, though, it was still the case that when I asked myself if I believed that Jesus was God and the answer came back no, and when it then also dawned on me that I didn't believe in God at all either, I could sense that I was uncovering an already-there truth. I knew that the moment I asked those big questions was not the moment my beliefs changed; it was just the moment I realized they already had. And that brings me back to what I sometimes feel so perplexed and uncertain about: When did the shift happen? Why so undetectably? When did my convictions fade and then disappear?

I suppose this book answers those questions for me—at least in part—in the descriptions of the many moments of doubt and struggle and strength-building that have taken up however many pages we've traversed so far. Looking back on my story, as far as I can tell, there wasn't one point in time when I was abruptly convinced that Christianity was not something I agreed with any longer. Rather, over years of skillfully (and desperately) avoiding cognitive dissonance, and through situation after situation where I felt the religion not agreeing with me, my beliefs eroded and dislodged until what I was holding onto was not actually faith but simply the only view of myself that I'd ever known.

Given the position in which I found myself on that day of self-examination, with a new and stunning understanding that my previous beliefs had dissipated at some point and the only part of my religion I had left was the now-hollow label of "Christian," I was faced with another set of big questions—namely, could I imagine myself as something else? Could I imagine myself separate from Christianity?

Somehow, sitting on that stucco porch, looking at those leaves, feeling the warmth of the sunshine that found its way through them, I knew that I could. I saw a life for myself on the other side of belief, and I came to see what my next and final step would have to be.

HOW TO LEAVE THE CHURCH

THERE ARE SO many reasons why people who were raised in the Christian church and continued their commitment to it into their adulthood don't ask themselves the big questions about what it is they believe—big questions that include whether and how the historical narrative they embrace is possible; questions about whether they personally feel it to be true. Asking these sorts of questions is a particularly scary step to take in a life like that because it means, potentially, admitting that you've been very wrong. And not just wrong about something like the best route to take to get to the airport or how to pronounce a word you've never heard anyone speak out loud before—wrong about the entire way you viewed the world, the measures by which you judged others (and yourself), and all the doctrine you so vehemently insisted was true in the face of anyone who called it into question.

Or, if such folks do ask themselves those big questions, it's usually done as something of an intellectual exercise, an entertaining game wherein assumptions are not actually challenged, and the fear of having wasted years being misguided about the nature of the universe is never truly faced. In my experience, even those Christians who are among the most liberal-minded and who pride themselves on doing some boat-rocking now and then do struggle to sincerely scrutinize their theism. They might reject certain versions of God—the fire-and-brimstone God, the prosperity gospel God, the paternalistic God—but so many aren't prepared to sit with the prospect that some kind of Christian God might not be real at all.

So, this step isn't just about asking the questions; it's about asking them in a particular way. A way that requires your willingness to put the very foundation of your faith on the line. A way that legitimately considers the possibility that the Christian story is not true. If you're anything like me, asking the questions in this way will take intentionality and practice, because genuinely probing the beliefs that you committed to oh so long ago is antithetical to the belief system itself. The church doesn't tend to allow for that level of skepticism from a true devotee—at least not the churches that I grew up in. It doesn't allow for the possibility of its own error. As a result, even into adulthood, I wasn't used to being open to whatever answer I came across. I wasn't used to using a scientific-type method on myself. You might not be either, and that's okay. This whole process is a long and difficult journey, but I can tell you from experience that if you're ready and willing to ask the big questions in this way, you're almost there.

"There," of course, means having left the church. "There" is—for me, anyway—freedom. It's freedom from having to continue pretending to believe what I no longer believe. Freedom from truncating myself in order to remain the person that those who knew me when I was younger expect me to still be. Freedom, also, from fear of divine judgment, and from the self-cannibalizing notion that my body and its desires are inherently wrong. Doesn't it sound nice? As far as I'm concerned, being free from the church is better than anything I ever got when I was in the church.

But I'm jumping ahead. We still have to wrap up this sixth step. And I should give it its full due, because while the seventh and final step is thrilling for a number of reasons, this penultimate one actually gets me most excited when I think of others taking it. After all, what could be more inspiring than the idea of someone discovering their own truth? I feel invigorated just thinking about someone like me, who was raised almost exclusively within one particular worldview and who sacrificed so much of themselves in order to be good by that limited measure, finally coming into the knowledge of what they themselves believe. I'm overjoyed for everyone this has happened to, and overjoyed for everyone to whom it's going to happen in the future.

Granted, it could be that what you discover when you ask yourself the big questions in good faith—questions like whether Jesus was actually God or whether there's a God at all—is that you do in fact believe the church's teachings, to one extent or another. You may find that you do personally and sincerely believe that there is a God, and that Jesus was the son of God and deserves to be worshipped as such. Or maybe you find that there are some aspects of the Christian narrative that, if you're being honest, you don't believe, but there are others that you do.

Whatever the particular combination of your convictions, that's alright. The point of this step isn't to convince yourself that there is no God; again, that would be just as bad as disingenuously convincing yourself that there is one if it meant going against your own judgment. The point is to bring whatever is heartfelt in you out into the light—to brush off the layers and layers of others' stories and their expectations and reveal to yourself what it is that you can say with a sense of integrity that you believe.

It takes courage, to be sure. It takes trusting that your opinions matter, which can be a tricky thing when you've been raised in an environment that says they don't. It takes recognizing that you might know yourself better than the pastors who've taught you and even the people who raised you, which can smack of pride to those of us who were taught that independent thinking is an affront to the Lord. Indeed, it might feel like you're risking literal hell to sincerely ask and answer these big questions. And I suppose that's true, in a way. But look how far you've come already. Look how many risks you've taken, consciously or not. Look how courageous you are.

If your journey's been anything like mine, and if you're in the place where you think you might be ready to ask these big questions, then you've already doubted the things you were taught. You've already been (and even stayed) angry with God. You've broken out of your comfort zone and experienced love and support from the people you were told were miserable sinners. You've braved a critical, researched study of the Bible. And, you've dared to open your eyes in church in order to fully face what it is you're participating in each time you gather with other believers to demonstrate your faith. You have what it takes to ask yourself the big questions, and you have what it takes to answer yourself honestly.

You also have what it takes to do what needs to be done next—to follow this journey to its natural conclusion, whatever that looks like for you. For me, it meant mustering the audacity to release the versions of myself that didn't apply anymore, even though they'd served me well in earning praise and comfort. It wasn't yet clear what I would lose or what I would gain in the process. Even now, I'm still learning. But something in me was compelled to see my quest through to the end, and I've never been prouder of a choice I've made before or since.

STEP 7
LET IT GO

After that revelatory day on the porch, I had some decisions to make. There was no denying what I'd discovered about myself. I couldn't un-realize my lack of belief; I couldn't un-encounter what I'd chosen to face. But untangling my life from what I thought I believed—what I used to believe, what I'd spent so many years saying I was—was a different story. What was I going to do about that?

I was still attending the Episcopal church at this point, and while I was no longer involved in that community in any leaderly capacity, the folks I saw there on a regular basis made up a more than trivial portion of my social life. Then there was the ritualistic aspect of church. Despite my theological hang-ups, I liked the regular contemplative moments, the collective singing, and the wisdom I found in the sermon every week. And of course there was the sentimental part: Church was something deeply known, deeply familiar. It was part of what created that warm nostalgic glow around certain celebrations and family traditions that I looked forward to each year because they reminded me of bright spots in my childhood.

Speaking of which, another concern—less immediate but still serious—was my family. I was living three hundred miles away from my parents, so it wasn't like I was going to be facing daily questions about my faith or pressure to continue acting like my beliefs were the same. But what would happen when I went home for the winter holidays, and we embarked on our annual trip to the Christmas Eve service at my aunt and uncle's church in the next city over? Would I refuse to go? Would I suck it up and fake being comfortable with an old-school gospel message for just one night? Would I pretend to agree with the worldview they all assumed I still had if it came up in conversation? I wasn't really concerned about being banished outright, but as someone who avoids conflict with my family like the plague, even the prospect of having to explain my new perspective on Christianity and deal with their potential disappointment or lack of understanding felt overwhelming.

One thing was certain, though: I couldn't keep going through the motions of being a Christian knowing that, in my heart, I didn't buy into its basic tenets anymore. Many people do, of course. I'm pretty sure there are plenty of church-going adults who don't personally believe what they're teaching the kids in Sunday school. I often wonder how much the people who taught me as a child, and even as a teenager, really believed. I assume folks like that keep attending for tradition's sake, or for the structure of it, or to keep up appearances. In more liberal congregations, like the Episcopal one I was still attending—physically if not in full spirit—I think there are also many people who might not believe that there is a literal God but who are comfortable taking the story as a metaphor and going on about the worship anyway.

For better or worse, neither of those situations felt tenable to me. I'd exhausted my ability to compartmentalize my feelings when it came to what was being taught in church, either explicitly through words or implicitly through the routine corporal demonstrations of devotion. Being in the position I was in—living away from my family, without a partner or children to consider, and not holding any position of responsibility within the church community—the only person I might have kept going for was myself, and it was clear that I'd reached a point where the frustrations outweighed the benefits.

Still, walking away from the church entirely was a big step—the biggest step so far—and I was hesitant to take it. Unlike allowing myself to sit with my doubts or really feel my anger, both of which were more passive in nature, this was something that I would have to initiate. I had to choose whether I was going to keep making my way through the motions of a Christian life. I had to choose to what extent I wanted to make this years-long internal process of leaving the church public—how I wanted to bring it all to a close.

I tried to imagine myself continuing to go to church indefinitely and continuing to refer to myself as a Christian, and just the thought of it seemed like a waking death. That couldn't be what anyone would want for me. After all, wasn't Jesus all about life? Not that I was actually turning to Jesus as the touchstone of wisdom for my decisions anymore, but the frame of reference I'd been using for decades wasn't something so easily sloughed off. Plus, I found it kind of delightfully ironic that the freedom through rebirth that Jesus said he offered was something I'd found in my rejection of the church's teachings rather than within them. In any case, holding on to what I'd always known was technically an option, but a depressing one.

The other option was, well, letting go. Leaving entirely. I tried to imagine that, too. I imagined sleeping in on Sunday mornings. I imagined finally giving away my small collection of Bibles and no longer bothering to pray. I imagined what it would feel like to meet someone new and, if it the topic came up in conversation, being able to say, "I'm not religious." What would I call myself instead? Atheism seemed too far-fetched for me at that point, but I thought agnosticism could work just fine. I imagined this post-Christianity, post-church life, and while it did feel strange and unfamiliar, it also felt right.

There was nothing I needed the church for anymore. There was no reason for me to keep the faith, as far as I could tell. All it did was stress me out and make me mad and rein me in from being my authentic self. It also kept me from loving myself, and though I probably wasn't fully conscious of it yet, that was the most destructive part of it all.

Yes, there would be things I would lose if I chose to leave. And I would need to find a way to cope with life's harsh blows that didn't involve crying out to an invisible, unresponsive god or gritting my teeth and waiting for the afterlife to come. But the hunger I had to be free of my now-hollow commitment to a religion that I couldn't justify to myself or others was stronger than the existential fear of what it would be like to truly be on my own.

I decided to open my hands and let it slip away.

THE FIRST THING that fell away was church attendance. One Sunday, I decided not to go, simply because I didn't want to. I wasn't sick, or too busy—I just thought I'd try out doing something else with my precious weekend hours. In the moment, I wasn't thinking of it as a permanent decision. I knew that if it felt wrong not to go and I really did want to return, I could.

Nevertheless, it turned out to be a positively refreshing morning. I took my time getting up and getting ready for the day. I brought a book to a coffee shop down the street and treated myself to a leisurely breakfast of French press coffee and a croissant with butter and jam.

As I sat at one of the cafe's sidewalk tables, enjoying the edges of the prenoon sun and watching strangers pass by on their way to who-knows-where, it struck me how many Sunday mornings—how many thousands of hours—I'd spent doing what I'd been told was good for my soul instead of what actually was. That's not to say that there weren't edifying aspects of church attendance. Hopefully I've made it clear that there was a lot I valued about the ritual. Still, I found that not going was better for me, especially once it was evident that I no longer saw the world through the Christian kaleidoscope I'd been using since I was small.

The next thing I did was give away most of my Bibles, as well as most of the theology books I'd collected over my two years in seminary. This part of the process came somewhat organically, as I ended up moving out of the Green House and into my own apartment not long after I decided to stop going to church. The move provided a convenient excuse to comb through my library and be intentional about what I wanted to go through the trouble of packing and hauling across town. For the most part, religious books didn't make the cut.

I did keep one Bible. It was a New American Standard translation that I'd purchased in college and taken with me all around the world. It had a decade's worth of notes in it; the leather cover was worn from years of my hands' pressure and sweat. Even so, I wasn't keeping it out of sentiment—well, not quite. For me, it felt like the last tangible connection to the religion I was ninety-nine percent certain I wanted to leave. But there was still that one percent of suspicion about my choice to de-convert, and getting rid of that particular Bible felt like a finalizing gesture that I wasn't ready to make just yet. So I put it in a drawer I rarely opened and told myself that if, in a year, I'd forgotten that it was even there, I'd know that it was time to let it go. Indeed, a little over a year later, it was gone.

Another thing I needed to actively release—the thing that was somehow both the most personal and the most public—was my identity as a Christian. That is, I needed to stop calling myself a Christian, and in some contexts I needed to say decidedly that I was no longer one. It's not that it was anybody's business, really, but given that I'd been so devout for so long, and the fact was that I no longer believed what I once did, there was no way to be both totally truthful in my existing relationships and silent about this monumental change in my life.

The easiest version of this part of the letting go process happened when I met new people. If the subject of religion or church or personal beliefs came up—if it was somehow relevant to the conversation—I could say that I used to be a Christian but was one no longer. I loved these moments, because just the act of saying that aloud, of saying, "I used to be a Christian," or, "I was raised Christian, but I don't believe in it anymore," helped make it real for me. Each time I declared it to be so, unbeknownst to whomever I was chatting with in the moment, my grip on that identity, on that old version of myself, loosened that much more. And, since most of the folks I was meeting for the first time at that point in my life were from outside of the church context, they were usually safe people to be decidedly non-Christian around. Those moments—and the acceptance I found—helped me practice being confident in my new worldview, which proved important when I found out how scary it was to tell believers who already knew me well about my change of heart.

I don't remember who among my Christian friends and family I brought it up with first. I do remember, however, the first time I felt the sting of a loved one's disappointment after revealing to them that I no longer believed. It was someone with whom I'd been close since high school, and someone I assumed had become more progressive in their own faith given how much we'd grown since then. Maybe I was naïve, but I went into the conversation expecting understanding and support; to my surprise, their response to my admission that I no longer believed in God was to say that they were sad the connection between us would be diminished—that we could no longer be as close, because our shared faith had been such a key part of the foundation of our friendship. All I could think was, *Isn't who I am as a person so much more important than the details of what I believe?* Perhaps my guard was down further than it should have been with that one.

We worked it out eventually, but from that point on, I was less explicit about my beliefs—or lack thereof—with folks whom I knew to be Christians and who assumed I was still one, too. If I was aware that someone else had gone on a journey of de-conversion similar to mine and wasn't into the church thing anymore, I might venture to bring it up. But, barring those moments when I was asked a direct question about my religious habits (moments that were, mercifully, rare) and despite my sincere desire to bring my whole self to every relationship that deserved it, I usually ended up avoiding the issue entirely.

I did, however, start writing about it. Publicly. On a blog. Which might seem a bit counterintuitive for someone who was so hesitant to be vocal about her departure from Christianity with the people she knew personally, but hear me out. At first it was anonymous. I shared the links to new posts on my various social media accounts, but my name was not attached to the posts on the blog itself, so only those people whom I told—or those who took the time to put the pieces together—knew I was the author.

Through my writing, I could both express the truth that I'd left the church and also tell the stories about what it was like growing up in that context and why I wanted to leave. And I could share my words with everyone in the world and no one in particular at the same time. The blog helped me discover what I really thought about all that had happened to me and helped me solidify for myself the fact that I was no longer a believer, all without feeling the pressure to defend my experiences or my choices to someone else's face. As I wrote and refined and published my reflections, I helped myself fully let go of that old identity I no longer wanted to hold onto anyway.

After a couple years of writing and posting incognito, when I knew I was ready to be recognized for my story—that is, when I felt confident in my new identity as a non-Christian and better prepared to face any debate or disappointment from friends and family that might come my way—I changed the settings on the blog so that my name appeared in the posts' bylines. That's how most of my family found out about my leaving the faith, years after I'd already completed the journey. By that time, though, my grasp on all that had made me a Christian in my own and others' eyes had been so fully released that I think it was fairly evident to all concerned that I was standing by my decision to take my life in a secular direction. Ultimately, few who knew me personally went to the trouble to push back. I also tried to make it evident that I was happy with my new life. That I actively wanted not to be a Christian anymore, and that I preferred walking away from the safety of the fold over trying to maintain what had turned into an unbearable faith.

Not everyone understood, of course. Surely, some of them still don't. But slowly, word got around to folks I was still in contact with via social media that I was a self-proclaimed ex-Christian, and people started treating me as such. Mostly, that meant saying things along the lines of, "I know you don't believe in God anymore, but I'll be praying for you," when I would post about some hardship I was going through. It was only strangers responding to my blog who would go out of their way to admonish me with statements like, "You were never a true believer," or, "You're going to hell and taking other people with you." Maybe the people I knew personally were thinking those things too, but they never confronted me about it. Even if they had—even if, someday, they do—I'd already taken my final step. I'd already left the church, and no matter what anyone had to say about it, the decision was for good.

WHILE IT CERTAINLY INVOLVED ITS share of pain, it's crucial to point out that my journey away from Christianity was a relatively safe trek compared to the path that some others must follow if they too want to leave. There were some things I lost along the way—things I had to grieve—but I am lucky to have parents and siblings whose faiths did not call for my excommunication from the family when they found out I was no longer a believer. Sadly, not everyone can say the same. Plus, living near a big city at the time of my de-conversion meant that I could find supportive communities (more than one, even) outside of the church. For some who live in rural towns or small cities in deeply Christian areas, there might not be any relationships available outside of the church bubble, and they might not have the resources to get to the places where they would be able to find and foster those connections.

I also think often about how lucky I am that I didn't get married before I changed my mind about God, despite how painful it was to feel weird and unloved in the midst of what I was terrified would be interminable singlehood. I know plenty of people who tied the knot before they had a chance to really question the beliefs with which they were raised, and who then had to figure out whether they could stay married—or who went ahead and decided they couldn't—after one or the other of them realized they wanted to leave the church and their spouse did not share in that revelation.

These stories are especially heartbreaking to me. Christianity already tends to be an exclusivist religion; add on to that this one pesky verse in the New Testament that warns against being "unequally yoked" with non-believers, and you get a situation where a difference in faith within a marriage usually isn't considered acceptable in church communities, especially evangelical ones. But neither is divorce. So the spouse who wants to be done with Christianity—who perhaps already knows that they don't really believe anymore—finds themselves in a situation where they will either have to pretend to be someone they aren't for the rest of their life or be blamed for destroying a family by following their heart. Worse yet, even if someone is willing to leave and sacrifice their reputation in order to choose a life of integrity over the charade, it might not be physically safe for them to do so.

All of these factors can make this last step particularly tricky—even dangerous—so I want to be clear that letting go does not have to involve outward demonstrations of inward de-conversion. A person can let go in their heart and mind even when they're not able to visibly disconnect from the fold. If there is no way for you to not go to church or to not engage with the Bible on a regular basis, and if declaring yourself to no longer be a Christian is even less of an option, that doesn't mean you can't complete your journey if you want to. Whatever it looks or feels like to release your old way of being in the world in your context is what you should do. After all, one of the primary lessons to be learned through this whole process is how to trust yourself. Only you know what it means for you to take the final step, and you don't owe anyone a performance.

IN MY EXPERIENCE, not trusting myself was a hard habit to break. It's been nearly a decade since I took this last step, and I still find myself inclined to pray in moments of panic. At first, when I was freshly de-converted and encountered a frightening or worrisome situation, I would find myself halfway through asking for help from the God I no longer believed in before I realized what I was doing. These days, the impulse to implore the Lord for aid has faded to a subtle twitch that I can usually identify before it manifests into actual action, like the remnants of an atrophied muscle memory learned for a sport I haven't played or cared about in ten years. Though the instinct is fading, I'm not sure if it will ever go away entirely.

I judged myself for this for a long time. I thought I had made a conscious decision to let go of prayer along with everything else. After all, if I no longer believed in God, what was the point of asking Him for support? I wondered if maybe I didn't know my own mind and heart as well as I thought I did, and perhaps, despite all the work I'd put into breaking away from a religion I no longer wanted to be a part of, I still believed in its tenets. I condemned myself as weak or stupid for not being able to do away with prayer once and for all, right away. Sometimes, I wondered if my involuntary drive to pray was a symptom of a mental health issue, and I worried for my own sanity.

It was a frightening cycle of thoughts to go through, but those thoughts led me to a deep self-examination for which I will be forever grateful. I was forced to ask myself why I prayed in the first place, even when I was a believer. Because if prayer was something that some part of me still wanted to do even when God was no longer a part of my worldview, then my reasons for engaging in it went beyond simply asking for help or offering thanks. That's what I figured, anyway, and I think I was right.

I won't take you through every detail of the path of self-analysis that I followed to come to an answer for why I kept praying. It's meandering and in some places beyond my ability to articulate. But the gist is that I found within myself an almost total lack of self-reliance. A striking absence of belief that I could handle what might come my way, even the stuff that was out of my control. Starting in early childhood, I'd been taught by the church not to trust myself, and, apparently, I did a very good job of taking that lesson to heart. My total inability to know about and wield the tools I had at my disposal to deal with life was so deep-seated that consciously rejecting the Christian narrative was just scratching the surface of what it meant for me to leave the church.

In other words, it was a lot easier to do away with my belief in God than it was to do away with my belief that I needed God. And all of those outward, visible actions—no longer going to church, giving away my Bibles, saying aloud that I wasn't a Christian anymore—turned out to be only part of what it meant for me to let go. My automatic response to intense stress or anxiety about a situation was to look for supernatural help, and that response was based on a feeling of helplessness. Like a young child who goes to the closest adult for aid when they don't know what to do, my immediate maneuver was to turn to my heavenly savior to fix things. Except, I was too old to be feeling so ill-equipped. When I asked myself why I really prayed, I discovered how little I found myself capable of being in charge of my own life, and how badly that needed to change. Once I started addressing the root issue by taking steps to build confidence in my ability to take care of myself, I found that my reflex to pray lessened in both force and frequency.

I also realized that I needed to give myself a little more grace as a brand-new ex-Christian. With all the indoctrination I'd received over the years and all the ways I'd molded my entire life around the church's teachings, there was no way this final step was going to be a totally clean break. It was unnecessary to judge myself for not doing it in a way that felt right. No one, human or god, was standing by waiting to dole out punishment. The whole point of leaving was to live life on my own terms; I was allowed to forgive myself for not living up to anyone's standards, including my own.

The concept of being allowed to do something is a tricky one in Christianity—especially the more conservative branches, like the evangelicalism in which I spent most of my religious life. It's about more than the rules and regulations congregants are told to abide by during their time on Earth. It's about free will. Technically, I was taught that humans have free will, that we are ultimately in charge of our own decisions and that, though God can see all possible outcomes and knows all that's happening in the world at any given moment, we are not being controlled by Him like marionettes on strings.

On the other hand, I was also taught that God, being all-powerful, can intervene in any given situation should He so choose. There are multiple stories in the Bible where the Lord shows up in some magical, even terrifying way to persuade an individual to do what He wants them to do. There's the classic burning bush scenario, of course, wherein God convinces Moses to go and rescue the Israelites from slavery in Egypt. In the New Testament, the Apostle Paul tells the story of how God appeared to him and blinded him with a bright light to prevent him from continuing to persecute Christians and to convince him of the fact that Jesus was indeed the Messiah. Though I never personally experienced God stopping me in my tracks with a miracle to get my attention, I know I prayed many times for Him to force someone else to do (or stop doing) something in order to nudge things closer to my vision of how a just and righteous world was supposed to be. I believed that was one of the main reasons for prayer, in fact: to beg God to interfere with the way things are going on Earth, both for His benefit and for mine.

I was also taught that, though any human is totally free to accept or reject the gospel, if a person should use their free will to choose not to admit that they are a sinner and turn to

Jesus for forgiveness, that decision will result in their being punished for all eternity. I can't count the number of pastors I've heard use this idea to explain that hell is just another way God cares for us. Over and over again, I was told that in His perfect, unconditional love, God will always let us make our own decision about our life's path—always let us exercise our own free will—even if it means we ultimately opt to be separated from Him and get stuck in infinite misery as a result.

Now, I don't know about you, but to me, these things do not sound like free will—they sound like only the illusion of it. To me, in fact, they sound like manipulation and abuse. That is, it sounds like the label of "free will" is given to our situation by the church to appease us while we are actually being compelled to abide by a specific religion's laws. If we are welcome to make whatever decisions we want *unless God feels like using us to change the course of history*, then are there not some serious limits to how far we're allowed to take this whole free will thing? Or, if the only choice a person has is between paradise and torture, but in order to get paradise they have to proclaim a very specific set of beliefs that they may or may not actually agree with, have they really been given agency? I mean, if you are committed to the idea that proclaiming belief in Jesus of Nazareth as your Lord and Savior is the one and only way to avoid agony in the afterlife and that's just the way it is, fine, but let's not be disingenuous with the idea that that narrative can somehow coexist with true self-determination.

As you can see, I get a little riled up about this subject. The reason I bring it up is that when you grow up in the church, particularly in more stringent churches, your so-called free will becomes a moot point because you quickly learn that what matters is not your personal autonomy (even though they say you have it) but your ability to discern and act on the will of God. And so, if you are like I was, continually seeking to be obedient in order to avoid displeasing the Lord, then you are constantly—obsessively, even—trying to figure out what He wants you to do in any given moment. The idea is to use your free will to choose God's will. Unfortunately, in the same way that a lack of trust in one's own abilities to handle adversity can create a dependence on prayer so chronic that it outlasts one's involvement in the church, this incessant checking-in with the divine to see if what you're doing is okay forms a habit of permission-seeking that can remain a part of one's personality even after one has realized there's nobody to seek permission from.

Knowing that's the case, if there's one piece of advice, one word of encouragement, I can offer to someone who's considering whether to take this final step, it's that you are allowed to do it. Again, what "it" looks like—what letting church and God and Christianity go means for you—will differ from person to person. It might involve literally leaving church and never picking up a Bible again. It might involve being vocal about the fact that you're no longer a believer and sharing stories about the harm that was done to you, intentionally or not, by the church and its teachings. Or, it might need to be limited to a decision that you've made inside your heart—a decision that no one else knows about yet and maybe never will. Whatever your version of letting it go is, you, dear one, are allowed to do it. You are allowed to make your own decisions. You are allowed to do what you want.

OF COURSE, so many things about this process are easier said than done. I've seen a lot of progressive-minded Christians take every other step in the journey—I've seen them walk right up to this line—and be unwilling or unable to cross it. For some, it's because they do actually want to stick with the church. They might reject the more patriarchal teachings about women and sexuality, as well as a capitalistic, prosperity-minded gospel, but they sincerely believe in God, and perhaps even in the divinity and salvific power of Jesus, so staying committed to Christianity makes sense for them. Or, even if they feel that all the doctrine and theology is up in the air and they're not sure what's real about the Bible, if any of it is, they still find that Christianity offers a comfort and rhythm that makes life easier and more enjoyable, so they happily choose to remain involved.

There are others, however, who have nothing to stick around for, who have no good reason to keep holding on, but who simply feel too scared to let go. There is the fear of no longer being what you've always been, of course, but beyond that, for many, there is the fear of doing the wrong thing. And for those who were taught since childhood that doing the wrong thing could mean incurring the ire of a God who's compelled to punish those who flaunt His will, it feels infinitely safer to bury the doubts and anger and inclination to leave and just stick with what you know—or what you've been told—is right. So they cling to church and keep the true state of their faith secret because the fear of what God might do to them if they leave feels more powerful than the desire to break free from what they've outgrown.

I'm only one person, and I certainly can't speak to what God—if God exists—will eventually do to or with any of us who choose to leave the church, but for my part, I can attest to the fact that I haven't experienced anything resembling vengeance, retribution, or wrath from above since I started identifying as a former Christian. If anything, I'm enjoying more personal growth and opportunity than ever before. I've certainly encountered my share of passionate believers who reach out to me to tell me that I'm working as an agent of Satan, but even more people have reached out to say that they too have never felt better since leaving the church.

All I can say is that for many of us once-zealous apostates, a lot of the fears that might have kept us holding on to the faith longer than we really wanted to have not yet proven true. Who knows what will happen after we die—that part remains a mystery, and probably always will as long as we find ourselves on this side of that great divide. But so far, God has done nothing to intimidate me into coming back or to punish me for leaving in the first place, which only makes me more confident that my years spent cowering in what I thought was His omnipresence were a mistake.

EVEN WHEN WE conquer the fear of punishment, we must face the inevitable anxiety of empty hands. If you let go, what will you have left? What's going to keep you occupied and anchored? Where will meaning and purpose come from, if not this narrative about a god who's in charge of the whole universe and wants to save it from destruction but needs our help? These are all fair points.

I've heard that one key to getting rid of bad habits is replacing them with good (or at least less harmful) ones. For instance, if I were to try to stop biting my fingernails—and I am always trying to stop biting my fingernails—I might keep a stress ball nearby so that when I get the urge, I can play with that instead of chewing my cuticles to bits. Replacing an entire worldview might be a little trickier, but I think the principle still holds, so it's worth considering what we can pick up at the same time that we're letting things go.

For me, first, there was the constant learning that I needed to sustain. I love learning. Something that endeared me to the Bible—and a big reason why Christianity had such appeal to me as a bookish teenager—was my sense that it was an endlessly study-able text. Granted, the fact that I found it to be a perpetual source of wisdom and fascinating information about the cosmos was largely thanks to how I learned to think of it as a child: perfect, holy, a piece of God Himself. But my love for it was organic, too. I saw the Bible as my primary connection to the Truth, as a font of never-ending revelation. When it finally lost its luster for me and I could no longer take it seriously as divinely inspired writing, though I wanted to put it out of my sight for all that it represented of my former life, I also found myself sad to lose such a faithful companion in my efforts to understand the world.

To address the void, I made a commitment to explore other avenues of truth—ones that I'd been convinced were insufficient because they were not Christian. I started reading about Buddhism. I studied as much as I could about tarot and chakras. I dove into philosophical and spiritual texts that would've been seen as dangerous in the churches where I grew up. Nothing ever became like what the Bible was to me in the sense of it being the one book to turn to time and time again. Never again did I consider a single document to be, for all intents and purposes, an instruction manual for life. But that's as it should be. There would be no point in letting the Bible go only to replace it with yet another idolized, narrow vision of the world. Instead, in its place, I took up the possibility of many perspectives, many worlds—options so vast that I was ashamed of how much time I'd wasted on a single book when I could have been learning about a gorgeous diversity of interpretations of life.

It was a similar story when I let go of attending church.

The hours spent at Sunday services had their purpose, but once I realized that I was showing up more out of perceived obligation than personal conviction, and that I was an independent adult who could do whatever she wanted with her weekend mornings, I felt somewhat embarrassed by the way I'd been allocating my time all those years. There was no lack of things to do with those hours—meaningful things—in lieu of Christian worship. Since Sunday mornings weren't typically conducive to social gathering for my non-church-going friends, especially if the night before had turned out to be eventful, I decided to replace "God" time with "me" time. I let myself sleep in and get ready for the day at whatever pace I wanted. I treated myself to breakfast at one of the handful of coffee shops that were within walking distance of where I lived, sitting and reading and people-watching until I felt like heading home and taking care of whatever tasks I needed to accomplish that day.

For folks who are preparing to let go of church but who have a lack of social ties outside of that community, maybe instead of Sunday morning solo time, you can take the opportunity to start exploring your own interests while also planting the seeds of new friendships. You could find a meetup in your area, or see if there are any opportunities to volunteer for a local community-serving organization during those hours. It might also be interesting to try out a different spiritual pursuit, like a meditation gathering. Just be careful that you're not simply replacing one sense of obligation with another. There are so many things to do with our lives besides going along with this one single tradition. The unfamiliar is naturally intimidating, but I promise, if you want to, you can find fulfillment elsewhere.

Another thing that's tricky to let go of, as I mentioned before, is prayer. Like I said, I found that it stuck to me no matter how I tried to pry myself away from it, or it away from me, like sap from a tree I'd once laid my hand against that no soap could cut through. A big part of processing my inability to simply let go of that particular aspect of Christian life was realizing the root of the compulsion. Along with that, though, I needed to figure out what to do instead: what habit I could replace it with that would help me divest from those compulsive pleas to a deity I no longer believed in. Knowing that what I was really struggling with was faith in myself, I decided that every time I noticed myself starting to ask God for help, I would make a list in my head of all of the things that I could do to help myself or others in that situation. Similarly, when I was worried about some scary situation that might happen but hadn't happened yet, rather than begging God to magically stop this frightening, hypothetical thing from occurring, I would take a deep breath, imagine the worst-case scenario, and then make a list of all the options I would have if that terrible thing ever came to be.

Beyond these prayers of supplication that popped up on an ad hoc basis in response to life's unforeseen circumstances, I also had a habit of just "spending time with God," as younger evangelical me would have said. I was committed to setting aside at least a little bit of time each day during which I would not only ask God for things but also express my gratitude, tell Him how great I thought He was, confess what I thought were my failures to live up to His standards, and get some questions and anxieties off my chest. To help fill that void once I was post-belief, and to practice releasing things I could not control a little more and perseverating on them a little less, I decided to try Buddhist meditation. Through that practice, I learned how to access a stillness and acceptance of the reality of the present moment that has been so much more helpful and healing than any version of Christian prayer I ever participated in.

No replacement habit I chose to practice was ever perfect, and none of them felt exactly the same as the behaviors I'd engaged in before. In fact, sometimes they felt downright awkward. Nevertheless, these actions helped make my life on the other side of belief a practical reality. They also worked exclusively from the outside in, which still left me to address perhaps the most daunting dilemma one comes to after finally mustering the courage to take this step despite the cost, despite the fear of stepping into the risky unknown. How does one replace an identity?

Unfortunately, I can't answer that for anyone else because I have yet to figure it out for myself. All I know is that there will be a vacuum there, that other identities will naturally rush in to try to take the place of "Christian" in your life, and that you will be tempted to claim them. For me, at first, as I said, I was particularly interested in Buddhism. After all I'd been through with Christianity, though, I was (and still am) wary of declaring myself an adherent to any one religion or belief system, no matter how far afield from my upbringing it seems to be. Because of that, I dabbled but never committed.

Then, a few years after my departure from the church was complete, when I began writing about the process on my blog, I discovered that there were small communities of former evangelical Christians who were finding each other online. Through the peculiar magic of social media, I built relationships with others who had a similar past, and I started to feel a sort of pride and belonging in our shared identity as ex-believers. However, I also started to feel myself drawn in by the gravitational pull of a kind of group zeal—one organized around a mutual (and very well justified) anger about this shared experience, a common wound—and I once again found myself becoming nervous about pigeon-holing myself, wary of being caught in a centripetal force that simplified all my thoughts and experiences down to a classification that, while not wrong, was far too easy. I also eventually realized that, while the commiseration was healing, I didn't want to spend my time thinking more about my past than my future, so at a certain point I made a choice to be conservative with how much of myself I invested in those spaces.

That's not to say that my natural inclination is to be a loner. On the contrary, the truth is that I am a person who loves being a part of a group. You might not know it from watching me, as I can be quiet and tend to avoid being the center of attention, but I am profoundly energized when I can sense that I'm connected to a vast network of relationships. I love feeling like I'm part of something special that's bigger than myself. Thanks to my experiences with the church, though, I'm now also very apprehensive about joining up for anything. I'm scared of getting pulled back into a mob mentality, of being manipulated through a shared passion into not thinking reasonably and critically about things. I'm also trepidatious about labels. They serve their purpose, of course, and can be useful to us if we stay aware of their limitations. Still, given the life I've led, it puts a bad taste in my mouth to say "I am X" or "I am Y" about nearly anything.

Considering all of that, when it comes to this idea of taking up a new identity to replace that of Christian, I'm not sure I'll feel comfortable holding on to a particular sense of myself so tightly ever again. I also don't know if that's a good or bad thing, or if it simply just is. It might be one of those situations where the absence is the presence—the scar the healing—like a redwood tree that's permanently hollowed out from a fire, but the gape is what lets you know that it managed to survive.

NO MATTER who you are or what the details of this journey have looked like for you, my guess is that taking this last step will feel a little like jumping out of a plane without a parachute. It did for me. Growing up in the church, I always heard adults say that it takes more faith to be an atheist than a Christian. When I first realized that I was indeed an atheist, I resented the adage, but maybe it's true. It's at least true that if you've been in the church for a long time and have been a sincere believer, it does take more faith to leave than to stay in it. To be blunt, it's fucking scary. But scary doesn't have to mean bad. And choosing to put your faith in yourself rather than a religious tradition that chafes against your better nature is not wrong, despite what the people who can't handle your truth might say. Let them talk. This is your life, and nobody knows better than you what the right move is for yourself in this moment.

As you decide on what that move is, though, there is one final thing that I must insist you believe. I know, I know—my whole thesis up to this point has been that you should believe what you want, what you feel is best and true for you. Nevertheless, I can't wrap up this step without making sure you understand this as a fact:

You are not alone.

There are a lot of people who have done the very thing you might be thinking of doing—who have actually left the church—and who are happy, not just in spite of leaving but because of it.

Others, including me, have gone before you into the mystery; others, myself included, have come out the other side, perhaps a little rattled but alright. Better than alright, in fact. We are thriving. And if you happen to find yourself here, all the way on the other side of indoctrination, a little flabbergasted but free, then it will be your turn to look back across the path you just travelled and let the folks behind you know that everything's going to be okay.

EPILOGUE

In a letter to the Christians of Galatia in what is now the country of Turkey, the apostle Paul wrote, "It is for freedom that Christ has set us free." The churches that shaped and sustained my faith throughout my life referenced this freedom—and this particular Bible verse—often. It was why we were all there, and what we used to try to convince others to come join us. It was what we used to convince ourselves that we had it better inside the church than out in the secular world.

But what was this freedom? In context, Paul's words have to do with his insistence that new gentile believers in Jesus as the Messiah did not need to follow Jewish law in order to officially become Christians. In his letter, he is saying that they are free from the burden of legalism, and that their faith is made real when it is demonstrated "through love." Sounds nice. Unfortunately, I did not find that kind of freedom in the Christianity with which I was raised.

In my Christianity, I had to believe that I was inherently sinful, and, as a woman, inherently restricted in my roles and responsibilities. I had to believe that God's default mode was punishment, and that this was somehow the same thing as unconditional love. I had to believe that sexuality was dangerous and dirty unless expressed in the context of a heterosexual, monogamous marriage involving two cisgender people (in which case, it was holy and beautiful). I had to believe in things that were not just mysterious but contradictory and irreconcilable with accepted scientific knowledge. I had to believe that the way I was raised was better and truer than any other worldview or culture.

Despite what all the preachers and Sunday school teachers and camp counselors and youth group leaders said about the freedom that Jesus offered, the truth is that I was chained down by my faith in multiple ways, and I didn't recognize the situation for what it was for a long time. Yes, there were things I was explicitly prohibited from participating in—so-called sinful things—but before I had much experience in the world, I assumed those rules were in my best interest and that I was better off for having followed them. As for the anxiety I felt about whether God would deem me worthy, waiting to see if He would answer my fevered prayers to help me or help the world—well, that kind of drama may not have been pleasant, but there was a certain masochistic appeal to it. Life was never boring when I was caught up in the Christian fantasy.

But again, I was not free. I was not free to follow my own heart's understanding of love, or even to change my mind about the workings of the universe as more information presented itself to me. The church told me that there was one right way to see the world, and that in the case where my own inclinations butted up against that vision, it was always going to be me who was wrong and the church who was correct.

At a certain point, I just couldn't take it anymore. When

the cracks in the Christian daydream began to show—which I assume they eventually will for anyone who's paying the slightest bit of attention—rather than ignoring them, I decided to try to peer through to the other side. What I saw there looked like actual liberation, and though the process of breaking out of and away from the church was scary and slow, what I felt when I was finally unfettered by religion was, I think, that delicious, refreshing freedom that I'd been hearing about since I was a child.

I know that this might be hard for those who are still committed Christians to believe, but I can say with absolute confidence that I've found more comfort in the absurdity of a godless universe than I ever did in the ordered, organized, everything's-already-worked-out Christian faith I inherited. When I believed in the God of my youth—the God who was somehow simultaneously all knowing, all powerful, and all good—the world as it is didn't make sense. It didn't make sense why so much injustice was happening if God was all three of those things. And the lack of sense was extremely, existentially stressful because I wasn't allowed to look at things any other way. I *had* to believe these things about God, and I *had* to reconcile them with what I saw happening in the world around me. It was a moral imperative, and yet I could never really do it.

The minute that God disappeared—the minute I chose to let Him go—it felt like I was breathing air for the first time. It was like when I got my first pair of glasses at sixteen years old and thought to myself, Is this what the world was supposed to look like this whole time? Is this what everyone else has been experiencing around me? I hadn't known I couldn't see well. I hadn't known there was a crisper, clearer vision of life just waiting to be had with a basic switch of the lens. Yet suddenly there I was, a whole new, religionless future ahead of me, and I couldn't wait to get started.

I WRITE about letting church go—whatever that means to you—as the final step in this process. The truth is, it's also the first step in a whole new journey. Once you've released your old mindset, your old habits, your old identity, you are in the very exciting position of being able to dream about what's next and not have your potential limited by tradition, obligation, or guilt. You can ask yourself what kind of career *you* want to have, rather than stressing out about whether you're living in line with some divine calling. You can choose friends and partners based on things like compatibility and emotional intelligence instead of assuming that relationships are God-ordained simply because they came your way. There's no end to the possibilities when it comes to what you can make of your post-church life.

That said, it would be unfair of me not to acknowledge a couple of things about the new stage in which you find yourself. The first is that being a formerly devout, in-it-with-your-whole-heart, Church-was-your-second-home evangelical Christian can bring its own version of shame. Especially if you've replaced your church community with one that is decidedly secular and liberal, you might be embarrassed by your former religious zeal. Perhaps you've heard the people around you make fun of evangelicals or deride the conservative worldview that often accompanies Christian belief. Even if you agree that the way you acted in your past was wrong, it can be difficult to be honest about the kind of life you used to live when you feel you might be judged for it. You might feel it best to hide who you were—and thus what partially shaped who you currently are. All I can say in response to that is, in my experience, even the people I know who are the most critical of Christianity have generally been fine with the realities of my past. If anything, I've found them to be fascinated by my story. It makes me wonder if my fear of rejection is based on the assumption that everyone outside the church world will be just as judgmental as everyone within it was.

One very specific way that my shame about my hard-core Christian background reared its ugly little head was when it came to dating. After I was done with the church, I did not want to date—and certainly did not want to marry—anyone who was a committed Christian. Yet I also feared that only someone who'd been as deep in the church as I was would be able to have compassion for all that I'd been through. I was terrified that, because of my past, there was no atheistic or agnostic, liberal-minded man who would want anything to do with me, yet that was exactly the kind of person I wanted to partner with long-term. The situation felt impossible, until it didn't.

I'm happy to report that the thing I feared most—namely, being unable to find a nonreligious partner who would accept, without suspicion, what a devout Christian I'd been—did not come to pass. On the contrary, I found a partner who, when early on in our relationship I asked him to name something he liked about me, said that he really admired the fact that I'd been able to change my mind about Christianity despite how fervent my involvement in the church had been. He said that it was a rare thing for someone to have the courage to make a shift like that, especially as an adult, and that he found it impressive. I'd never thought of my journey as admirable. Thanks to him, I was able to see my past not as a burden but as an asset.

I suspect that this acceptance and appreciation for our

stories is more prevalent than we former believers might fear. Not necessarily from the folks who are still in the fold, of course—it's likely that many of them will be unwilling or unable to recognize our departure from the church as a legitimate choice. But outside of that bubble, I think, I hope, you'll find that you will be welcomed with open arms when you step into the world that exists beyond the boundaries that fundamentalism told you to never cross if you wanted to survive. I think the people over here, where I've found myself for the last decade or so, will be happy to see you. I know I will.

The other thing that must be reiterated is the set of advantages I had in my journey away from the church, because these are advantages that continue to aid me as I embrace my new, church-free path. As I've mentioned before, my parents are relatively open-minded people as far as Christians go, and I've had the luck of living in geographic locations where Christianity is not the default culture. On top of that, my precollege education being mostly public meant that I was exposed to content unfettered by the church's interest (as much as that can be true for public education in the United States). My ability to do well in traditional schooling also afforded me the opportunity to get out of my hometown, away from the folks who'd known me since I was a baby, and to experiment with crafting the life I wanted to live rather than the life I knew other people thought I should live.

As I said at the start, all I can speak to is my own experience, and there is no denying that I've had my fair share of both privilege and luck. Still, I do believe that freedom from the various bonds of the church—from the emotional, intellectual, and even physical constraints of Christianity—is possible for those who want it. More importantly, it is deserved. You deserve to follow the path that feels good and true to you. You deserve to know yourself and to trust yourself accordingly. You deserve to love yourself, and you deserve to be able to share your love with others in a way that is unlimited by arbitrary understandings of who's in and who's out, who's sinning and who's been forgiven for their sins.

Now, if it so happens that you have found and continue to find that truth and love and self-acceptance from within the church, that's fine. The only thing I ask is that you believe us former Christians when we say that we're so much happier now that we're not carrying around the burden of an ancient law and its strange, manipulative modern manifestations. As for me, I can say with confidence—in fact, I've never said anything with more confidence—that leaving the church was the best decision I've ever made for myself. I want every Christian who intends to stay a Christian to hear that, and I want every Christian who's thinking of maybe leaving the church to hear it too.

ACKNOWLEDGEMENTS

This book would not exist without the care and support of so many people, some of whom are alluded to in its pages. I'm thankful to my parents who, regardless of any pressure or criticism from the religious communities they were a part of, championed education, travel, and all manner of creative pursuits. I'm indebted to my siblings for their support as well —at times our paths have differed and at times they've converged, but we have always been able to find each other when it counts.

To my Green House family, thank you for welcoming me when I needed a new place to bloom. My profound gratitude goes out to Monica, Wolffie, Kimberly (who confirmed my suspicion that these steps should be turned into a book when I first shared them with her), and Libby. I have so many years of precious memories with each of you; I hope you all know how much I love you. Thank you also to Sharon, who, in addition to being a faithful friend, makes me a better writer and helped make this a much better book. To Jennifer, thank you for being one of my first readers and most ardent cheerleaders. And to my Portland community, which I'm privileged to say is so abundant that I can't name all of you individually, it was and is an honor to share life with you.

I will be forever grateful to John Mabry at Apocryphile Press for his eagerness to publish this book. It was no small feat to find the publisher who both understood its significance and was willing to jump into the controversy with me. Working with Apocryphile has been a blessing and a pleasure.

I must mention my sweet girl Nellie, a feral mutt my husband and I adopted into our little family shortly after we got married, who slept at my feet over hundreds of early mornings spent working on this manuscript. She passed away not long after I signed my publishing contract, and I sense something of the cycle of life in that. I am a better person for having loved her.

Finally, to Nate. I am constantly trying to find words to express how I feel about our partnership. I think the most accurate thing I can say, which I also mean as the very highest praise, is that I could not be more content. You love me with action and integrity, you insist that I pursue my goals (and make sacrifices to ensure I can), and you help me see myself as remarkable. Thank you.

www.ingramcontent.com/pod-product-compliance
Lightning Source LLC
Chambersburg PA
CBHW020330170426
43200CB00006B/340